Civilizations East and West:
A Memorial Volume for Benjamin Nelson

This volume constitutes
Number 10 (1983) and Number 11 (1984) of the

COMPARATIVE CIVILIZATIONS REVIEW

Civilizations
East and West:

A Memorial Volume For
BENJAMIN NELSON

edited by
E. V. Walter, Vytautas Kavolis, Edmund Leites
and Marie Coleman Nelson

Humanities Press
Atlantic Highlands, N. J. 07716

First published in 1985 in the United States of America by
Humanities Press Inc., Atlantic Highlands, NJ 07716

Library of Congress Cataloging in Publication Data
Main entry under title:

Civilizations East and West.

"This volume constitutes number 10 (1983) and number 11 (1984) of the
Comparative civilizations review"—Half t.p.
    1. East and West—Addresses, essays, lectures.   2. Civilization, Occidental—
Addresses, essays, lectures.   3. Nelson, Benjamin, 1911-1977.   I. Nelson,
Benjamin, 1911-1977.   II. Walter, E. V. (Eugene Victor), 1925-
CB251.C568   1984   909'.09821   84-569
ISBN 0-391-03065-5

MANUFACTURED IN THE UNITED STATES OF AMERICA

Table of Contents

Preface

The idea of this book emerged more than a dozen years ago. Conversation with Benjamin Nelson teemed with intellectual projects and schemes of exploration, but he feared that time would run out before he made his work available to the world. One of the editors, moved by his eloquence, promised him a festschrift. Later, in meetings at his summer place in Montauk, a small community of friends and students pursued the idea of making a collection of essays bringing together his work and their work. But he died in 1977, and the festschrift seasoned into a *Denkschrift*.

The German word *Denkschrift* means a written memorial, but it also suggests a record of thought. The stir wherever Nelson went is the excitement caused by a remarkable man of thought. The editors want to keep alive the ideas of Benjamin Nelson himself and thoughts about his life and work as well.

Four of us who were close to him spontaneously formed an editorial group. Many writers responded to our call for papers with very interesting essays, but financial limitations these days demand a lean book, and with great regret we were forced to turn away some excellent contributions.

Publication of this volume is made possible by a subsidy from the International Society for the Comparative Study of Civilizations (ISCSC) and by support from the Benjamin Nelson Foundation and Dickinson College. Carroll J. Bourg copyedited the manuscript. We are grateful for Simon Silverman's personal interest in the book.

"Systems of Spiritual Direction" is reprinted with permission from *Criterion* 11, No. 3 (Spring 1972), pp. 13–17. "Games of Life and Dances of Death" is reprinted with permission from *The Phenomenon of Death*, ed. by Edith Wyschogrod (New York: Harper & Row, 1973), pp. 113–31. Marie Coleman Nelson's essay, "Ben Nelson: A Personal Memoir," originally included in this volume, was published instead as the lead article in a special memorial issue of *Social Research*, Vol. 49, No. 3 (Autumn 1982), pp. 578–88.

Editors and Contributors

Louis Dumont is Directeur d'études at l'École des Hautes Études en Sciences Sociales in Paris.

Vytautas Kavolis is Professor of Comparative Civilizations and Sociology at Dickinson College. He was President of the ISCSC from 1977 to 1983.

Edmund Leites is Associate Professor of Philosophy at Queens College of the City University of New York. He was a Vice President of the ISCSC from 1977 to 1983.

Marie Coleman Nelson, after a career in New York City as a psychoanalyst, editor, and writer, moved to Kenya. She lives in Nairobi and directs a counseling center.

Nathan Sivin is Professor of Chinese Culture and the History of Science at the University of Pennsylvania.

Charles Trinkaus is Professor of History at the University of Michigan.

Eugene Victor Walter is a writer who lives in the Boston area. He taught sociology and other subjects at several universities, and was a colleague of Benjamin Nelson at the University of Minnesota and the New School for Social Research.

Edith Wyschogrod is Professor of Philosophy at Queens College of the City University of New York.

Part I

COMPARATIVE CIVILIZATIONS

1. The Civilized Mind

E. V. Walter

The ancient Alexandrians enjoyed making lists of The Seven Sages, selecting wise men regarded as the most important thinkers of the ancient world. Perhaps they did it in the spirit of sports fans today, imagining all-star teams or hall-of-fame heroes. The ancient lists varied, but some names—notably Solon and Thales—appeared on virtually all of them. In our time, the reputation of Benjamin Nelson has a way of inspiring similar lists. Mention his name in some academic circles, or among some publishers and editors, and you will hear him exalted and compared with the great. One social scientist refers to him as one of the four greatest intellects of his time. An anthropologist says that Nelson "was one of the most important generative minds of the twentieth century." Talcott Parsons wrote in a letter to Marie Coleman Nelson, "The more I think about his work and my association with him, the more I feel that Ben was one of the notable figures in his generation. He certainly contributed greatly to the enrichment of my professional life over a considerable period of years. I shall always treasure the memory of my association with him." Another prominent sociologist and a well-known philosopher both observed that Nelson was the only person they knew who could have been another Durkheim or Weber. A distinguished historian writes, "his influence was so comprehensive and continuous that it seems to be alive and potently operating quite apart from the personal destiny of its subject."

Nelson's personal influence remains no less important than his intellectual stature. He never wanted a pedestal, but insisted on standing in the midst of us. We all knew him as "Ben." Our feelings about him continued to mix intimate friendship with the highest respect for the breadth and depth of his learning and for the power of his mind. We took his presence for granted as long as he stayed part of our familiar, everyday experience. Yet, we felt his greatness and knew him as a paradigm for the life of the mind.

Ben stays with many of us in the memory of walks and talks that were transformed by the power of his historical imagination. To walk with Ben was to step into a timeless time of everywhen and to share his vision of "the contemporaneity of the noncontemporaneous and the noncontemporaneity of the contemporaneous." The business of life was a series of interruptions in a conversation started years ago. If he made a visit to our city and we met him at the airport, between the moment we picked up his luggage and the time we reached the parking lot, we were deep in the 14th century.

Strolling with him in the streets of New York or Chicago or in Harvard Square changed our experience of urban life, making us perceive in a new way the rhythm and flow of the city. Sometimes, after a late seminar and extended conversation at the New School for Social Research, on the uptown bus to his old apartment in the upper west side of Manhattan, he would show us that late at night the bus changed into a droshky plunging through the streets. Under his gaze, the faces of the passengers—few at that hour—transformed into characters out of Dostoevsky. If we rode the subway with him in the morning, he would buy the *New York Times*, and we might hear a lecture on the meaning and history of "news." Ben cherished but transcended his early experience as a journalist. For him, information about recent events published in the morning paper was never "news" in the sense of a superficial, ephemeral report. He was fond of the word "tidings," which is larger than "news." Information about things that occur in time. Tidings are manifestations, reflecting the deeper rhythms of human thought and action. As a reader of newspapers, Ben remained to the end of his days, an "Abelard of the New York Times"—a distinction, we shall see, conferred early in his career.

For some of us, he stood for what he called "Free Social Science"; for others, intellectual and cultural history; for still others, the unity of the sciences. These interests only begin to name what he represents: medieval history; social theory; the culture of economic institutions; the interrelationships of literature, drama, and social life; psychoanalysis and culture; the significance of Weber, Durkheim, and Freud; the origins of the modern world; comparative studies of many kinds: religions, theologies, sciences, civilization patterns, structures of consciousness. . . . His work teems with perspectives and "fields," but identifying them does not do justice to the unities in his writing. In his last years, he worked toward establishing foundations for the independent study of comparative civilizations, and also toward transforming sociology through a perspective he drew from the histories of civilizations.

His authorship as a whole is beginning to attract attention in Europe as well as in the United States. In 1977, the year he died, *Der Ursprung der*

Moderne, a volume selecting and translating some of his papers, appeared in Germany. In 1981, Toby Huff, one of his devoted students, compiled a more inclusive American edition of writings by Nelson: *On the Roads to Modernity: Conscience, Science, and Civilizations* (Totowa, New Jersey: Rowman & Littlefield).

Over a wide range of scholarship, his influence continues to manifest itself, as three recent examples from sociology, philosophy, and literature will show. Guenther Roth and Wolfgang Schluchter dedicate their book on Max Weber to the memory of Benjamin Nelson. Alan Donagan writes in the preface to his book on moral theory that "Benjamin N. Nelson, then a colleague at Minnesota, introduced me to moral theology and to the history of casuistry in Christianity." And in an extensive literary essay on *The Merchant of Venice,* Marc Shell acknowledges his debt to Nelson's book, *The Idea of Usury.*[1]

Many thinkers change and grow by shedding their previous interests, but Nelson did not live that way. On the contrary, he deepened, widened, and enriched his intellectual matrix to expand the meaning and value of his early thoughts. A sketch of his academic biography reveals the steady development of early interests within an evolving cognitive framework.

Born in New York City in 1911, he was graduated from De Witt Clinton High School in 1927 and entered City College, where he did no distinguished work until his junior year. Public speaking stands out as his best field—until the "eleventh hour," when he discovered intellectual history in his senior year. Until then, he put all his energies into public speaking and into student journalism. The CCNY yearbook reveals him deeply involved in the work of the newspaper all of his college years. In addition, he served as a student correspondent for the *New York Times,* covering topics of religion and taking a special interest in sermons. He visited churches throughout the city, and especially liked to hear Roman Catholic sermons. He managed the varsity debating team, served on the student council, helped to organize social events such as "class night," enjoyed a reputation as an excellent dancer, and was voted the "most sophisticated" member of the senior class. He joined his friends in memorable protests against a notoriously reactionary college administration.

In his junior year, he studied philosophy, enrolling in two classes with Morris Cohen, but never completed the work for those courses. In the autobiographical essay included as Number 3 in this volume, Nelson tells us that Cohen's philosophy of law course initiated the "first decisive steps" on his journey of the mind. Still, Taylor Stoehr—the biographer and editor of Paul Goodman, who has studied lives and works of Goodman's circle of friends—detects another inspiration as well. In the fall of 1930, Ben enrolled in the first history class to excite him: a serious course in intellectual history offered by Walther Brandt, called History of the Renaissance, which included Paul Goodman and Lewis Feuer as fellow students. He helped to reestablish a moribund organization called "Phrenocosmia," which turned into a small group of serious under-graduates who read philosophical papers to one another. *Microcosm*, the college yearbook, which assigned a motto to each member of the graduating class, named Benjamin Nelson: "Abelard—of the New York Times." As we have already observed, even at the end of his life the epithet remained wise and appropriate.

He left City College already at work on the subject of usury, suggested, he tells us, by a chapter in W. J. Ashley's work on economic history. He went to Columbia to study history, where he completed both graduate degrees with both the thesis and the dissertation exploring medieval attitudes toward usury, campaigns against it, and programs of restitution for ill-gotten gains from usury. He read everything, ferreted out the most inaccessible sources, collected arcane documents such as original medieval bills of lading, and made himself a specialist—without doubt one of the world's leading authorities on the history of usury. His Ph.D. dissertation is the definitive work on restitution for usury in the Middle Ages, but it is immense, remaining unpublished in the Columbia University archives. Charles Trinkaus, an historian and an old friend of his, believes that "Ben's finest scholarship was contained in those typescript volumes." Since Columbia will not grant a doctoral degree unless the dissertation is published, Ben decided to publish a shorter book—but it turned out to be another study: not on the restitution for usury, but *The Idea of Usury*. This volume, published in 1949, shows that he was not merely a specialist, but a thinker for whom the putative boundaries of the social sciences were not barriers. He remained a historian, giving contextual explanations, yet went beyond history by finding explanations for the context that illuminated the subject. In the epilogue to *The Idea of Usury*, he tells us how, "at the eleventh hour," the larger framework grew clear in his mind.

Though he entered graduate school in 1931, Nelson's first publication waited until 1944, and the first work on a subject beyond usury did not appear until 1951. Where was Ben during this latency period? His old friends would probably reply, "In the stacks."

But he loved to be interrupted—to be fetched out of the library stacks for coffee and conversation. In the 1930s, Paul Goodman, Mike Liben, and Gene Thumin would seek him out regularly, and together they made up the core of a "Saturday night club," a durable group ranging from a dozen to sixty people, who assembled every week for serious discussion and for relaxation. Ben still loved to dance. He also wrote a music column. On Sundays, right through the middle of the 1930s, Ben and a few friends could often be found in the Goodman household, where Alice, Paul's sister, made dinner for them.

They referred to his studies as "The Brother and the Other," and Taylor Stoehr suggests that this close circle of friends was the social matrix for one of Ben's major ideas. Marie Coleman Nelson calls attention to the centrality of the fraternal relationships in Ben's family as well, and the informal fraternity of his personal circle during the years at CCNY and Columbia may have helped to shape the theoretical constructs in *The Idea of Usury*. Not to speak of his later ideas about the historical importance of sworn bands of brothers in cities and civilizations, as well as his keen interest in comparative histories of fraternization.

His friends marvelled at the range and intensity of his scholarly interests. Meyer Reinhold, the classical historian, recalls one occasion when a group of friends at Columbia were having lunch, expecting Ben to join them, and he came in excited and breathless. He explained his late arrival by saying, "I could not put down the new *History of Amsterdam* that just came into the library. It's a splendid work." Someone asked if it were a brief monograph, and Ben replied casually, "No. It's in twenty volumes."

Nelson received the M.A. in 1933 and the Ph.D. in 1944, both from Columbia University and both in history. From 1935 to 1944 he worked as a part-time history instructor in CCNY and in other municipal colleges. In 1945 he married Eleanor Rackow, and left New York for an appointment as Assistant Professor of History and Social Sciences in the College of the University of Chicago, where he taught for three years in the general social science program. In 1948 he moved to Minneapolis to work as Co-chairman of the interdisciplinary Social Science Program and as chairman of the European Heritage Sequence in the Humanities Program at the University of Minnesota. The years at Chicago and Minnesota were the middle epoch of his intellectual life. No longer identified as a specialist in the history of usury, he distinguished himself as a "free social scientist" who made history the matrix of generalizations. In the period 1950–54, three crucial works appeared: "The Moralities of Thought and the Logics of Action"; "The Future of Illusions"; and the interdisciplinary textbook, *Personality—Work—Community*, put together by Donald Calhoun, Arthur Naftalin, Benjamin Nelson, Andreas Papandreou, and Mulford Q. Sibley, with the assistance of the junior faculty in the Social Science Program.

Sibley remained at Minnesota teaching political theory; Calhoun moved to Miami, where he teaches sociology; Naftalin served as Mayor of Minneapolis; and in 1981 Papandreou was elected Prime Minister of Greece. Given the political, intellectual, and personality differences in this team, one marvels that they ever managed to work together, but they organized a profound, imaginative, wide-ranging selection of readings, wrote an important original text to go with them, and administered an exciting teaching program. Junior members of the Minnesota social-science faculty shaped in that crucible, helping to assemble the book and teach the classes, testify with pleasure three decades later that working in the program turned out to be one of the most important formative experiences of their intellectual lives. David Copperman, his assistant, remembers Nelson's remarkable style of teaching. In the course on "Personality," he refused to introduce technical terms such as "oedipus complex." Instead, he would begin a class by leaning over confidentially and, in a dramatic stage whisper, ask: "Does anyone here have a mother? And a father? . . . "

In those years at Minnesota, the campus simmered in heuristic energy. The spirit of the place conjured a community of inquirers who shared in imagination an adventure in common with the wealthy young men of ancient Athens, who had spent sleepless nights following the argument where it led, as well as with the young beggars of medieval Europe, who had lived in rags, on crusts of bread while they plundered the universities of wisdom. Nelson stood at the center of energy storms, lecturing, quarreling, debating, tirelessly persuasive, sharing his learning which seemed to have no limits. He had a way of engaging the minds of advanced graduate students from many different departments, meeting regularly, conversing with them as peers, and pursuing a subject intensely with them for months and years.

At Minnesota, he revealed the qualities that Edmund Leites memorialized almost three decades later, after Nelson's death:

> He was personally difficult, but what a generous mind! He was always ready to give intellectually. In a deep way he really believed, as few do, in the community of thinkers: he felt most comfortable in that setting and did much to make it real. And there was so much to be generous about! I signal two features of his intellectual character: first, it was dialectical; he sought to find the truth in the opposing view, which would complement the truth already known. So, to historians, he spoke as a sociologist and psychologist; to sociologists, as a historian; to theologians, as a historian and sociologist; and to social scientists in general, as a theologian of sorts. To Protestants, he could speak as a Catholic, so much so that Daniel Day Williams, of Union Theological Seminary, once angrily told Ben that he ought to receive the red hat from the Pope, he had done so much for the Roman Church. Some thought he had a Jesuit formation (we who knew of his early years on Tiffany Street in the Bronx knew better). To Catholics, he could speak as a Protestant; to Christians in general, as a Jew; and to Jews, as a Christian.[2]

In November 1950, a symposium which Nelson later referred to as "Conflict in the Social Order" occupied everyone's attention. It generated unforgettable excitement, and for each session over a three-day period, the lecture hall filled with crowds standing in the aisles while people outside strained to get near the room. Cooperman, who was a graduate student at the time, recalls the charged atmosphere in the hall, the "white-hot attention" focused on the speakers, the hushed standing audience, the intense exchange of question and answer after the lectures. The crowd refused to leave, and when the custodians finally managed to clear them out and close the hall, throngs drifted to cafés and other places that would hold them to continue discussion far into the night. At first, the series dwelled on the events and prospects of the Cold War, but the lectures and discussions moved to larger problems in war and peace, to the great political issues, to perennial questions of philosophy, and to the histories of civilizations. Nelson presented his paper, "The Moralities of Thought and the Logics of Action."

This paper raised Nelson's interest in casuistry to a new level of generalization, beyond the subject of usury, and he never ceased exploring the relationship between "rational analysis and moral activity." The processes by which humans struggled with the predicaments of social life, and in the West the progressive rationalization in the logics of decision, he remained convinced, linked science, social science, the humanities, and the moral life. A concise article on "Casuistry" by Nelson was included in the *Encyclopaedia Britannica* in 1963. The last paper he ever wrote—never delivered but prepared for the conference at Freiburg—concluded with reflections on the importance of formal casuistry for Western jurisprudence and moral theology.

In the "Conflict" symposium at Minnesota, Nelson delivered another paper, subsequently published as "The Future of Illusions" by the journal, *Psychoanalysis*, in 1954, reprinted in the Columbia University textbook, *Man in Contemporary Society*, Vol. 2, and in two more anthologies afterward. In this essay, he explored some collective dreams and irrational myths, offering his "historic reveries" to warn that fantasies emerging from the psychomoral disintegration of communities, nations, and societies will continue to threaten the world with violence "until the peoples of the world manage to discover new ways of defining their expectations and scaling their values." The social delusions he traced with erudite alarm grew out of deep convulsions caused by "the evident incapacity of our society to achieve patterns of integration which artfully orchestrate the multitude of conflicting wants, needs, and interests which men and groups in the modern world have come to experience." The remaining alternatives seemed to be anomic disorder or totalitarian control. He explained:

The patterns of integration which once appeared to have afforded a tolerable measure of consensus or stability have evidently collapsed and men seek in the midst of violence to fabricate new ones. Since society cannot function without the presence of spirit, men will insist on collectively worshipping idols rather than suffer the agonies of rootlessness and despair. Where subtle and satisfying forms of organic solidarity are unavailable, men will seek to escape chaos by adopting or imposing the yoke of mechanism.

He argued that strenuous efforts were needed to discover "new ways of living without a surfeit of delusion." In East and West humans would have to "live meaningful lives, without continually embracing over-mastering myths which drive them on relentlessly to the achievement of unobtainable goals." He concluded:

Humanity has no chance to endure if society will not learn in this eleventh hour to become *humane*—to build fit habitations for humans—that is, natural persons, neither demons nor angels, but men with all their perfections and imperfections, wedded to time but not lost to eternity.

In this paper, he suggested that inquirers might proceed in the spirit of Freud to look for the source of deeprooted delusion "in the nuclear experiences of men when they were children in the bosoms of their families." His publications in the 1950s reveal a profound, abiding interest in the writings of Sigmund Freud, and he launched a program to extend Freudian perspectives in the social sciences. After the new journal, *Psychoanalysis*, published "The Future of Illusions" in 1954, he continued writing about the work of Freud and the psychoanalytic movement, producing at least two dozen essays or reviews on the subject.

Later, the meaning of Freud changed in Nelson's writing. Instead of understanding the psyche as a compound of instinctual drives and family experiences, Nelson thought of it as an intricate synthesis of cultural, societal, and personal elements, as well as the precipitate of historical experiences. An analysis of the mind, he believed, lays bare some of the central moral dilemmas of Western civilization. He opposed invariant, universal concepts of personality, frequently arguing that "ego" was not the same in all times and places. He preferred a comparative historical perspective. He wanted to write about psyches, selves, and persons in a way that revealed their genesis within historical processes. The matrix of the family, then, remained too limited for his growing perspective. As he observed in 1965, "stereotyped applications of Freudian principles of symbolism and metapsychology are now increasingly felt to have brought us to an impasse." Freud's work, he believed, should be used to unravel the symbolic structures of consciousness and conscience, and to lead the way to a depth-historical phenomenology of minds in their sociocultural settings.

Nelson preferred to see individual pathologies in the larger setting of cultural malaise, and he wanted to find the structural determinants of identity crises and the social causes of anomie. The essay in which he develops a scheme for working in this manner, "Actors, Directors, Roles, Cues, Meanings, Identities" (1964) appears in *On the Roads to Modernity*, ed. by Huff. In that essay, he concluded:

> The way forward seems to require the recovery of certain lost accents of Durkheim's original design which had connected *anomic suicide* with lacks of integration within *as well as* among the central coordinating systems—the cultural, social, *and* personality systems. In this spirit we found ourselves construing cultures as dramatic designs, defensive elaborations, directive systems and symbol economies, (p. 31).

Cultures were to be understood as symbolic designs, coordinating systems that organized what to perceive, to feel, to do, to believe, to wonder at, to emulate. Alienation and anomie reigned when these frames of existence, expression, and reference went out of phase. Then rhyme and reason vanished from the world.

The first half of the 1950s was a transitional period: his first marriage ended in 1951, he moved to New York City to deal with medical problems, then taught for a year in the Contemporary Civilization program at Columbia, and returned briefly to Minnesota, where interdisciplinary social science continued perilously, under siege by the conventional departments. 1956; his 45th year, inaugurated his epoch of settled maturity—the last two decades of his life. He returned to New York permanently, taking a post that for the first time formally identified him as a sociologist, although he always retained a connection to history on the one hand and to interdisciplinary studies on the other hand. From 1956 to 1959 at Hofstra University he worked as Professor of History and Sociology, Chairman of the Department of Sociology and Anthropology, as well as Chairman of the graduate program in integrated sciences. Then for the next six years: Professor of Sociology and History, and Chairman of the Department of Sociology and Anthropology, State University of New York at Stony Brook. In 1966 he moved to the position he occupied until his death: Professor of Sociology and History in the Graduate

Faculty of the New School for Social Research, as well as the Director of a unit in the interdisciplinary program offering the Master of Arts in Liberal Studies.

In 1959, he married Marie Coleman, editor of the journal *Psychoanalysis*, and one of the inner circle of the National Psychological Association for Psychoanalysis, an organization of medical and nonmedical psychoanalysts which had originally formed under the leadership of Theodor Reik. Their literary partnership began in 1957, when they wrote an essay on "paradigmatic psychotherapy."[3] Ben remained an advisory editor of *Psychoanalysis*, which later acquired *The Psychoanalytic Review* and continued publication under this title. He organized a feature called "Adventures in Ideas," and edited or helped to edit a number of special issues of the journal. Altogether, he edited around ten volumes relevant to psychoanalysis or the significance of Freud, produced by *Psychoanalysis* and other publishers.

The late 1950s then found him established in the pattern of his most productive years: carrying editorial responsibilities for the journal as well as for publishers such as Meridian and Harper, illuminating the work of great writers, teaching sociology, administering academic programs, and writing extensively in a way that preserved the inherent connections of sociology, history, psychoanalysis, religion, and all the sciences that explored human thought and action. He was co-founder and, for many years, Senior Advisory Editor of the Harper Torchbooks, as well as Editor of two series of books: The Library of Religion and Culture as well as Researches in the Social, Cultural and Behavioral Sciences.

In 1958, he published his first essay explicitly on the subject of civilization, in collaboration with Charles Trinkaus. Their joint essay, originally read to the Columbia University Seminar on the Renaissance, appeared as the introduction to the Harper Torchback edition of Jacob Burckhardt, *The Civilization of the Renaissance in Italy*. It concludes with a statement that links history with the dynamics of selfhood:

> Western man has irrevocably been cast out—has cast himself out—of a childlike world of enchantment and undividedness. Since the days of his exile (or was it withdrawal?) he has been wandering the world. Wherever he goes he is readily recognized since he bears a burden for everyone to see—the burden of selfhood. The ego is at once his sign of Cain and his crown of glory.
>
> To seek to put off this burden by whatever device is to wish to reverse the irreversible. Everyman must stumble forward through unending labyrinths without ever finding a quiet haven or a journey's end. So to devise as not to be convulsed from within or

from without by the fateful heritage of selfhood; so to invest the ambiguous legacy as not to engender spiritual chaos or "mechanical petrifaction"—these are the grim mandates which were once laid upon the men of the Renaissance and which are now laid upon us who are their heirs.

The heirs of the Renaissance received another legacy as well. In addresses delivered around this time, Nelson urged that the multiple crises of our time demanded a movement of renewal. Scholars, he felt, have the special responsibility of pursuing "what the great historian Jacob Burckhardt once ascribed to the Italian Renaissance: the *rediscovery of man, nature, and the world.*"

In 1962, in a brief comment on an article by Edward Grant, "Hypotheses in Late Medieval and Early Modern Physics," written in *Daedalus*, Nelson published for the first time a line of inquiry that extended to the history of science his work on casuistry. He suggested that western religion was the historical matrix of modern science. The pioneers were seeking new foundations of knowledge and belief, he argued, and the basis of scientific inquiry—including the idea of probability—did not grow out of cosmology or physics, but developed from moral theory and philosophy. The dialectic of moral decision had worked out rules and procedures for testing and interpreting all kinds of knowledge and belief. "Without exception, all the originators of modern science and philosophy were intent on establishing (subjective) certitudes on the basis of (objective) certainties, moral and physical as well as mathematical, and in overthrowing the probabilist 'conjecturalism' of the learned." In 1965 and 1967 he expanded the investigation in two essays on the origins of modern science which appear in Part III of the volume edited by Huff. In the 1970s, the line of inquiry took its final form as a comparative differential investigation of sciences in the context of their civilizations. Here once again he found support in the classic studies of Max Weber but went further to explore the work of Joseph Needham.

Ceaseless reflection on the work of Weber caused changes in Nelson's thinking. In 1964, exactly a decade after "The Future of Illusions" first appeared in print, he published a brief statement, "In Defense of Max Weber," in *Encounter*, the first of about twenty essays he was to write explicitly about Weber's authorship. From about this time, the spirit of Max Weber pervaded his work. Though he never lost interest in Freud, Weber replaced him as the writer who dominated Nelson's intellectual life. Yet he insisted that Weber should be linked with the work of some other significant writers: notably, the legal historian, Henry Sumner Maine, and the French sociologists, Emile Durkheim and Marcel Mauss.

In the 1970s, Nelson's scholarly interests converged in working out *civilization analysis,* a discipline that would seek the common ground of the humanities and the social sciences in studying symbolic designs of the largest scale as active forces in their social settings.

In the spring of 1977, Nelson occupied his last academic post. He returned to Minnesota after two decades, as a Visiting Professor. In letters he reported that he "had a wonderful time in Minnesota," and that it was an occasion of "very warm reunion." Before returning to New York, he gave a public lecture on "The New Science of Civilizational Analysis: Vico, Mauss, Weber, and Today."

In the past he had often mentioned mandates and legacies from the Middle Ages and from the Renaissance. Now, in conversations with Peter Petzling, he clarified his latest interests and made suggestions we may interpret as a mandate and legacy to us.

He still spoke of great rationales and symbolic guidance systems, but wanted to inspire scholars and teams of workers to carry out research of an empirical nature—to discover how people actually do live, act, and think in the context of civilization patterns. He called the inquiry "the historical phenomenologies of experience and expression."

He had occasionally mentioned a social metaphysic of space and movement, but the notion begins to clarify and to grow more tangible. Nelson and Petzling glimpsed the beginnings of a line of inquiry. How— in the perspective of civilizations—does space get shaped and movement patterned according to symbolic guidance systems? Can the figuration of space and movement be codified and examined in their relation to rationales?

He mistrusted the abstractions of philosophical phenomenology and instead kept insisting on the *historical* phenomenologies of experience and expression. He felt that research of this nature would add evidence to his theoretical scheme, give substance to his program, endowing "civilizational analysis" with more currency in the academic world. Petzling felt that their conversations and the correspondence that followed were full of urgency and the sense of mission.

Ben was also excited about scholarly writing in Germany reinterpreting the life and work of Max Weber, especially the recent controversy about the erotic component—or its suppression—in Weber's thinking. The question leads to the larger issue of the role of *eros* in civilization. According to Petzling, the discussion raised questions about the rationales of *eros* and scholarship around the turn of the century in Germany and about the claims to authority of both *eros* and scholarship.

Ben kept wondering about the deeper meaning of the attacks on Max Weber, not only the political opposition, but the psychocultural critiques as well. From a civilizational perspective, he asked, what are the intellectual and emotional foundations of the revisionist movement seeking to reinterpret Weber's life and work? The issue has large implications, suggesting the possibility of great civilizational changes in the relation between erotic experience and the life of reason.

In the 1950 "Conflict" symposium at Minnesota, Nelson talked about the dynamics of romantic love in Western civilization. The theme remained an abiding interest, and in his last heuristic effort, he was still pursuing the trail of *eros* in the articulation of rationales. According to Petzling's impression of Ben's agenda in the summer of 1977, he intended to contact social scientists in Konstanz and gather responses to Nicolas Sombart's recent and controversial writing on the erotic dimension in Weber's work. Then he probably intended to make an inquiry in Freiburg about some of Weber's unpublished letters. But he never reached Freiburg.

Having delivered his ultimate lecture in Gottlieben in Switzerland, on Lake Constance, at a conference on Max Weber, he was intending to present a paper in Freiburg on Law and Tradition, but in the brief interval between conferences went to Tübingen to visit Friedrich Tenbruck.

Professor Tenbruck described Nelson's last days in a letter to Marie Nelson, from which the following is extracted:

> We met in Gottlieben, Switzerland, for a conference on Max Weber. As usual, Ben's paper was an impressive performance. The conference kept us busy and excited about Max Weber, sometimes in the company of Talcott Parsons, Reinhard Bendix or Gunther Roth, yet we found time for more personal exchanges. . . . [When he arrived in Tübingen] we put him up in our guest apartment which he knew [from an earlier visit]. . . . Ben was in good health and a lively mood all the time. There was no indication of fatigue. . . . He felt very much at home and enjoyed himself and us. . . .
>
> Some scholars objectify their intellectual personality and substance entirely in their publications. For Ben, his publications were a mere sample of his mind, and that is why they need to be interpreted, and not merely collected. . . . While Ben and I mostly talked very seriously about scholarly matters, our most rewarding conversations went beyond, where the vision that sustains publications reigns. In those days in September, we both had the feeling of an unreserved meeting of the minds and selves. And while we thus felt at one and were even making plans for joint work in the future, none of us had a foreboding that we would never meet again.

On September 17, Mrs. Tenbruck drove him to the station and helped him into the train to Freiburg. He died of a heart attack on the train.

Nelson's autobiographical essay, "Systems of Spiritual Direction," included in this volume, tells us how he understood his own spiritual direction. It also shows the connections in his personal intellectual history—linking his eras as a historian, free social scientist, and pioneer in the study of comparative civilizations. The concluding paragraph marks the direction of his last few years.

He left a large community of friends, students, and readers with lives profoundly touched by his work and his personality. Some of the contributors to this memorial volume—as well as some of its readers—will continue in the direction he marked out, advancing Nelson's program of inquiry. Others will proceed in their own way—some perhaps in directions he never intended or approved—but grateful for his insights, leads, and stimulation.

We treasure his work as we cherished him, and his writing appears in this volume as he liked to live—in the midst of us.

His intellectual life survives as part of our minds.

NOTES

1. Guenther Roth and Wolfgang Schluchter, *Max Weber's Vision of History: Ethics and Methods* (University of California Press, 1979). Alan Donagan, *The Theory of Morality* (University of Chicago Press, 1977). Marc Shell, "The Wether and the Ewe: Verbal Usury in *The Merchant of Venice*," *Kenyon Review* 1 (1979):75–92, new series.

2. *Psychoanalytic Review* 65 (1978):201.

3. *Psychoanalysis* 5 (1957):28–44.

2. Nelson's Legacy of Comparative Studies

Vytautas Kavolis

In the early seventies, Benjamin Nelson concluded a brief autobiographical statement by pointing in a new direction:

> Recently...I have become curious about several questions related to my growing interest in the comparative study of civilizations and of intercivilizational relations. Does the concept "conscience" give us any clue as to some of the differences in the distinctive patterns of development in various parts of the world? What are the relations between the structures of conscience and the tumultuous sociocultural processes of the 20th century across the world?...it is necessary to work one's way back through questions of this sort if we hope to work toward a basic foundation for sociology, history, and psychology and anthropology...we are now obliged to do a massive amount of work to get anywhere near these questions.[1]

The beginning of an autobiography reveals assumptions about what must exist (or occur) when the life of an individual commences its changes into a meaningful story. An autobiographical ending suggests what an individual has been transformed into by his passage through the machinery of his life, what his life signifies to him at the point when he is ready to leave it, as a finished (but perhaps, in later autobiographies, revisable) text, to others. Having begun with "a question for which I haven't really ever found an answer" (how he became a medievalist), Benjamin Nelson characteristically concluded with a reformulation of his old European questions in new and expanded frameworks. The old themes of conscience, work (both as necessity and as hope), and going back in order to advance to more "basic foundations" are now restated in a manner requiring a comparative study of civilizations.

The International Society for the Comparative Study of Civilizations, originally founded under the leadership of Pitirim A. Sorokin and mainly active in Europe, was revived at a meeting of the American Association for the Advancement of Science in Philadelphia, December 29, 1971. Nelson served as its president until the spring of 1977, taking a particular interest in involving comparative civilizational studies with all of the most vital intellectual developments and the most perplexing predicaments of the life of the time.

He considered the global studies of whole civilizations in the manner of Oswald Spengler and Arnold Toynbee to be dangerously speculative and likely to produce distorted images of the particularity of the historical experience of each civilization, a clear sense for which is what ultimately mattered. A more fruitful approach, he thought, would be to focus on particular analytical issues or processes of crucial significance to humanity, as well as to the various social and humanistic disciplines, and to study them in depth both within their own civilizational setting and in comparative civilizational perspective. It is in this manner that a reliable understanding of whole civilizations and of their historical trajectories, as well as the essential qualities of "being civilized," would eventually emerge, although we are not yet at the point for fruitful syntheses of this scope. This approach to comparative civilizational studies came to be known as the *civilization-analytic* perspective.

At the inception of his presidency of the ISCSC, Nelson co-authored with Vytautas Kavolis a programmatic statement, presented at a meeting of the American Association for the Advancement of Science in Washington on December 29, 1972. In this "inventory and statement" on "comparative and civilizational perspectives in the social sciences and humanities," the main approaches toward comparative studies were reviewed and criticized. Nelson preferred two of the eight "horizons" presented and explored. One was "the comparative study of *institutions* and '*symbolic designs*' against the backgrounds of determinate civilizational settings." The other was "the comparative study of the histories, sociologies, psychologies of civilizational complexes and processes as these are perceived and work in the settings of intercivilizational relations and encounters."

In the part of the statement he wrote, Nelson urged: "It is only as we see the civilizational complexes in the crucibles of intercultural process that we can perceive the distinctive thrusts and patternings of different civilizational and societal structures."

The two approaches he considered most promising:

> . . . describe ways of studying all sociocultural processes and issues within a distinctive *civilization-analytic* perspective which proves

preferable on general intellectual grounds (comprehensiveness, depth, compactness) to existing horizons and approaches in history, anthropology, sociology. The comparative depth-historical study of process and pattern in *civilizational perspective* offers great advantages over current varieties of structuralism, structural functionalism, schematic Marxism, phenomenology, inductivist empiricism, and so on.

The statement concludes with a more detailed specification of the main elements, as then perceived, of the civilization-analytic perspective.[2]

Nelson would speak of the "comparative historical differential sociology of sociocultural processes and civilizational complexes" and of "a polyphonic depth history and sociology of cultural expression and experience." Another name, "anthroposociology," he sometimes expanded in conversation into "psychohistorical anthroposociology," in search of a way of stating plainly where the movement stood among the academic disciplines.

Names were important to Nelson, and these shifts are clues to a characteristic quality of his speech in general. He kept talking about old concerns in renewed interpretative languages, seeking continuously to extend the range and appeal of his cognitive thrust. Each linguistic shift revealed or suggested new elements, angles of vision, possibilities. But the shifts were not systematically explained, the implications of changes in the rhetoric rarely spelled out in explicit detail. Nelson's sensitivity to the flows of subjective experience and its cultural expression made him averse to systematizing. He would systematize only when he went to battle. And he would go to battle usually when he saw the theory of culture inadequately developed by others.

Inadequacies in the theories of culture sooner or later proved to derive from insufficient discrimination between particular symbolic designs, as they have been shaped by particular peoples in the particular historical settings of their life. This insufficient discrimination, lack of nuance in approaching historical realities resulted in what he felt were the truly Satanic sins of contemporary social science—*schematism* and *uniformitarianism*, that is, the invention of abstract conceptual typologies without much perceptual content, and the search for generalizations about human behavior that would hold for all men and women at all times, independent of the particular histories of their institutions and their souls.

The social sciences which adopted these orientations Ben Nelson considered superficial, capable of grasping only the specious. The "depth-historical" understanding which he sought meant, first, a search for the shared symbolic structures underlying both human conduct and the most sophisticated symbolic formulations of a civilization and, second, a watchfulness for fundamental shifts of these structures in the crucibles of cultural struggles and encounters between civilizations.

There were the eternal polyphonies of *axial assumptions and rationales; cultural logics, ontologies, and epistemologies; dramatic designs; structures of consciousness and sensibility; systems of spiritual guidance; symbolic technologies; forensic frameworks; evidential canons; compelling metaphors*—indeed, compelling metaphors *all*. To understand these symbolic configurations in their actual workings was to become aware of their diversity, flux, and interpenetration in concrete historical settings. He discussed organizing a journal of comparative civilizational studies, to be named *In Process*. It appeared, after his death, as *Comparative Civilizations Review* (1978—).

He described his "sense of the sociological," in a particularly revealing manner, as deriving from "a predicamental vision," "the sense that people everywhere, whatever the form and structure of their arrangements, inexorably find themselves in the midst of predicaments which call forth urgent responses in the way of passions, actions, efforts to achieve mastery and control through multiple forms of affiliation, organization, imposition and imputation." (It is perhaps not accidental that Ben Nelson lists "passions," presumably in the dual sense of intensity of emotion and suffering in which the term is used in the Christian and Romantic traditions, *first* among the responses to "predicaments.") He added, in *Sociological Analysis,* a key phrase from his final conception of sociology: "I see no way of doing sociology without clearly relating to the structures of *existence* of peoples, the structures of their *experience*, and the structures of their *expressions*."[3] For him, they were all symbolic structures, languages for organizing both thought and action.

Nelson saw diverse kinds of symbolic structures everywhere, but, unlike the structures which the structuralists see, *these* structures were fluid, if viewed over time, and rigorously prescriptive, utterly clear in their definition at any given time. All the fluidities had a way of ending up as structures, and indeed one had to be firmly locked into some symbolic design to experience "meaning." But there was more personal meaning in the structures believed to be fictional than in the structures known to be necessary: "mummery . . . alone confers significance on acts which might otherwise seem pointless and futile."[4] It is not the profound that needs a mask but that which, without a mask, could be neither profound nor indeed human.

There is, in Ben Nelson's anthroposociology, a peculiar mix of a medieval and early-modern need for decisive symbolic guidance, and a sense of human existence as the continuous staging and dismantling of various kinds of spectacles, none of which seemed to be meaningless. Life is theater and, in our times, he thought, a grotesque one, in which the games of life, to which the magnificent rituals of earlier times have been reduced, turn out to be indistinguishable from the dances of death—but it is nevertheless to be analyzed rationally and lived in accordance with clearly defined canons of responsibility, a position I have tended to perceive as that of a late Roman intellectual.

As a scholar, Ben Nelson was an apprentice to the master puppeteer, the spontaneous spectacle of culture, seeking an exact understanding of how *each* string in *all* the diverse performances operates. The strings were the particular lines of movement of faiths, of sciences, of technologies, of laws, and the more immediate expressions of experience in literatures, and only if they have left an intellectually impressive record and have had practical effects on the historical scale were they worthy of being closely watched. Only the "world-historical" nations seemed to matter in the movements of civilizations.

He was unusually sensitive to the sources of modernity in the spiritual movements of the twelfth to the seventeenth centuries. But he also responded quickly to the most recent innovations of thought in a variety of fields. He wrote more powerfully on Jean Genet than on Max Weber and considered Paul Valéry rather than Arnold Toynbee a master civilization analyst. He would have made a fine literary critic. One of his most exhilarating articles is an inventory of analytical methods for the history of psychiatry.

"Ben knew more about civilization than anyone I ever encountered," wrote his long-time colleague at the New School, and intellectual antagonist, anthropologist Stanley Diamond.[5] He has left exemplary civilization-analytic studies of key ideas and idea complexes in Western civilization: the self and conscience, probability and certitude, the categories of *eros, logos, nomos,* and *polis,* the emergence of universal standards in economic transactions and international relations, and the little appendix on friendship. In the comparative study of civilizations, he had time to outline a distinctive approach. He wrote the dramatic statement on "Civilizational Complexes and Intercivilizational Encounters," developed his typology of sacro-magical, faith-, and rationalized structures of consciousness, dissected the differential trajectories of the histories of science in China and the West. In his work on the structures of consciousness, Nelson has been particularly concerned with the social contexts of *insight*—the historical conditions which have favored (or blocked) the breakthroughs to the faith- and rationalized structures; less with the social contexts of *plausibility*—the historical conditions which sustain the vitality of a particular structure of consciousness once it has been elaborated. His studies centered not on descriptive comparisons but on theoretical issues central to explaining the differential trajectories of modernity in various parts of the world.

In these studies, he grappled with some of the key issues in the problematics of civilization analysis, such as: Why did something of universal significance emerge or become potent only in a particular civilization? How come that the same problems have been subjected by different parts of humanity to differing procedures and given diverse solutions? Why are some major intellectual or institutional patterns borrowed across civilizational lines and others are not? Why does something which works well at one time cease to work at another? How is comparative quietude broken by effervescences, efflorescences, and aggressions?

Nelson did much to advance civilization analysis as a general methodology for studying any theoretically significant social or humanistic issue with full attention, first, to the cross-civilizational range of alternative ways for dealing with it; second, to the interdependence of particular solutions within the largest sociocultural configuration of which they constitute understandable components; and third, to the changes over time in the design and workings of particular civilizational structures in the concrete sociohistorical settings in which they were located.

The relationship of his theoretically sophisticated work to sociological theory as currently constituted has remained problematic. He was engaged in reconciling Max Weber's processual with Emile Durkheim's structural conception of society and concerned to incorporate into this larger synthesis all that was vital in later historical, philosophic, and psychoanalytic thought. But his main contribution to a comparative-civilizational sociology has been that of generating a pre-theoretical matrix, a pluralistic repertoire of symbolic frames for capturing the essential constituents of the great wealth of evidence on the diverse modes of consciousness and currents of sensibility that a close historical investigation reveals in any civilization. Benjamin Nelson has done more than formulate a general theory of civilizations to which his name could be attached; he has provided us with an evocative rhetoric which, instead of limiting our attention to the questions he has raised, activates our own scholarship by making alive the immense variety of symbolic designs that must be identified and closely examined in doing serious work in sociology, anthropology, intellectual history, studies of religion and of philosophy and, he hoped, psychiatry.

Ben Nelson has created a language that makes it possible to talk about *all* of the symbolic structures which tradition provides (or we create) for interpreting experiences and guiding actions, but with particular attention to those which focus on moral and intellectual responsibility. From beginning to end he has been concerned with symbolic configurations transcending those of a single society or language (though the structures he found usually emerged in Greco-Latinized forms). He has greatly increased our capacity to describe in precise and evocative ways particular cultures and their changes arising from encounters and conflicts between clusters of ideas.

He had his limitations. Not in his general statements of intentions, but in his actual cross-civilizational studies, he tended to remain Western-centered. Ben Nelson did not glorify the West, particularly the contemporary West, but, in all its mortifications (and, for him, we became more real precisely in our mortifications), he still considered it, with Max Weber, as having produced the only history of universal significance. He tended to see other civilizations as answering Western questions and as problematic in terms of what they, by Western standards, lacked: notions of universal brotherhood in India, modern science in China, individual conscience in the world of Islam. On these issues, he could be hard on the experts.

As a man of the book and the theatre, Nelson could not quite take mythology, that ancient, organic unity of reason and emotion, seriously as a legitimate part of modernity. His love belonged to rationality, his tenderness to language: he was quite extraordinary in the precision of his evocations, terribly suspicious if not fearful of the messiness of inexact emotions, experiences without structure, wildly utopian dreams. He was curious about the metaphoric passions unleashed by the various social and cultural upheavals of his later years, the possibility, around 1970, of encountering on New York's Fifth Avenue, as he left his New School office, walking impersonations of the different historical epochs and cultural movements he had studied. But he was repelled by the lack of a "reality principle" in most of this "revolutionary" and "counter-cultural" creativity. There was much of a romantic consciousness in his conception of sociology, held ardently in check by sobriety and the spirit of scholarship.

The spirit in which he sought renewal of "our civilization—Occidental and Oriental, Western and Eastern, alike" was that of literate, tragedy-sensitive rationalism and an adult, that is, illusionless, disenchanted responsibility shared by all mature minds, regardless of their ideological commitments, transcending in importance the lines of division between religion and secularity, radicalism and conservatism. For an adult to be "childlike" was the worst possible transgression against the requirement for integrity. Nowhere in Ben's work does one find the slightest trace of sympathy for the lost paradise of childhood.

And now we must ask: How central is the final achievement of Benjamin Nelson to his chosen fields, history and sociology, and to the other disciplines to which he offered it as a guide? Will these disciplines respond by embracing the "wider frameworks" of symbolic understanding that would save us equally from schematisms, whether scientific or ideological, provincialisms uneducable or principial, the enthusiasms and the burlesques? Or will a "new science of civilization analysis," a homeless discipline, have to be founded or perhaps recovered once again? Would Benjamin Nelson have had to confess, a few years hence, that he failed in teaching sociologists, as he did declare in the auto-biographical statement cited earlier that he had failed in enlightening psychoanalysts?

The reviewers have judged Benjamin Nelson's work to be of major significance in reconstituting the dynamic cultural frameworks which a genuinely global sociology requires, in conceiving of comparative sociology as a differential analytical history of consciousness. But while Nelson's influence is spreading and his spirit—in its imaginative precision and faithfulness to evidence—is alive to challenge others, he has not left a viable school of sociology working on the agenda he has set. Perhaps his repetitive agenda-formulating efforts were self-defeating. Nelson was eager for followers, anxious about their faithfulness, and he did occasionally use his own analytical categories in the manner of magical incantations. But there has never been anything but sobriety in his vision.

The basic reason for the uncertain future of what Ben Nelson did after *The Idea of Usury* is that his approach impressed too many people as a peculiar kind of history of meanings: too structural for historians, too intellectual for sociologists, unyielding in its intangibilities. Sociologists still need to do detailed studies to understand how social conduct generates itself out of the categories and symbolic matrices provided by intellectual histories, and by the struggles of men and women to make their histories meaningful. But that is now an inheritance of the friends and critics of Benjamin Nelson.

NOTES

1. Benjamin Nelson, "Systems of Spiritual Direction," reprinted in this volume, p. 33.

2. Reprinted in part in *Sociological Analysis* 35 (1974):129–141, as well as in *On the Roads to Modernity* (ed. by Toby E. Huff), pp. 230–243.

3. Symposium on his "Civilizational Complexes and Intercivilizational Encounters," *Sociological Analysis* 35 (1974):131.

4. "*The Balcony* and Parisian Existentialism," *Tulane Drama Review* 7 (1963):72.

5. *Social Research* 45 (1978):4.

3. Systems of Spiritual Direction

Benjamin Nelson

Professor Don Browning of the Divinity School chaired an afternoon seminar after a morning lecture by Professor Benjamin Nelson. He pointed to the graciousness with which the guest had consented to speak informally and to reveal something of the connections he himself made between his work in medieval history, Max Weber, and psychoanalysis. He posed the questions: "How does it happen that a medievalist can get us interested in systems of spiritual direction, both ancient and modern, as you have done? What is at stake in the questions you have put to yourself—and to us? Why does this theme occupy your interests?" What follows is Professor Nelson's reply:

Your wonderful directness compels me to remark that from where I sit there seems to be a prior question—prior to the one you put to me. It is a question for which I haven't really ever found an answer that is satisfactory to any of my friends and students. How did I (Benjamin Nelson) ever become a medievalist in the first place?

Well, I hadn't the faintest idea that the journey on which I was engaged could carry me along that rugged road. My first decisive steps occurred in these realms as an undergraduate in a course in the Philosophy of Law I took with Prof. Morris Raphael Cohen at C.C.N.Y. Prof. Cohen is perhaps known to some for his work here at the University of Chicago. I chanced to read a passage in Holdsworth's *History of English Law* which referred to the fact that it hadn't always been taken for granted by all people that every individual had an absolute right to use and abuse with respect to what he called his own. That struck me as unusually interesting and I looked at the notes and noticed as references two books: W. E. H. Lecky's *History of the Rise of Rationalism* and another work by W. J. Ashley, *An Introduction to English Economic Theory and Legislation.* I proceeded to read the works in order to get some sort of clue as to what this sentence meant and what its base was.

I guess that as I read I was overcome by a notion especially strong in Ashley, that once upon a time, in an era almost wholly unknown to me except through some undergraduate courses which had not indeed contained this emphasis, it had occurred to men to suppose that they could fashion a world that answered to the highest demands of the moral impulse. This was an astonishing idea, and I felt that I had to find out how they came to think they could reconcile their differences and what kinds of instrumentalities they applied to make sure that they were going along a track that made sense. How were they able to assure others that they were achieving some actualization of the ideal.

Now, it just happened that Ashley gave us a chapter entitled "The Canonist Doctrine of Usury." I didn't know anything at the time about usury (though over the years more than one friend and colleague has suspected that I have had some connection with the practice!). When I read Ashley's chapter, I discover another fascinating fact, namely, that in the Middle Ages people had worked out an elaborate structure, a framework of moral and juridical government for almost every sort of activity, experience, or relation that they would have.

Such was my outlook when I came to Columbia University for graduate work. My professor there had other plans for me. He wanted me to work on the Manuscript (Ms) 609 Toulouse with a view to establishing that those who had been charged with heresy were indeed men who were intent upon the assertion of the right of free enterprise, which was opposed by the Church. But I was already too deep into analysis of the work on usury to take that suggestion at face value, because I knew that the Church as such did not prohibit free enterprise or intend to stand in its way, at least not clearly or unambiguously. But it did do something else, and that was to prohibit the manifest practice of usury as the Church defined it. Indeed, it did require that those who had taken high interest or those who had been apprehended in the act, who were manifest practitioners, would be put under the obligation to make restitution.

That is where I started. Then I went forward with studies in a terrain that at that time was very uncultivated, and for which, unhappily as I was to find, there were few mentors. Now the situation is wholly different. We have an extraordinarily excellent group of people, including many very young ones, who are thoroughly equipped in the sources and substantive doctrine of the Romano-canonical jurisprudence of the Middle Ages. Anyhow, I did write a dissertation on the *Restitution of Usury*. By the time I finished it, though, I had become aware of something. I was working on another book: *The Idea of Usury: From Tribal Brotherhood to Universal Otherhood*. In the course of working out that book I was struck by the fact that for several thousand years there had been an unambiguous prohibition of usury between brothers. The texts referred to were always the same. Then in the era called the Reformation, with Luther and Calvin, there occurred the most extraordinary change in the terms and contexts of the discussion. I had fixed on a passage, Deuteronomy 23:19,20, and had decided to study the history of the exegesis of that passage with the utmost care and detail.

The book issuing from this research wasn't acknowledged by American church historians as stating the whole truth unambiguously, but was rather better received in Europe among those who had a wider knowledge of the central structures of conscience and consciousness—I use the word "conscience" now for the first time—sensibility, the terms of reference for self, society and so on that had evolved and yet were very active elements in the life of religious communities.

Again and again in the course of my life, I was to discover that I never really knew what I was doing until I had done it. Thus, it was only as I was finishing *The Idea of Usury* that I recognized that it might have been wise to have done it altogether differently. Thus my book has an epilogue which said that now that the book was done I was aware of the fact that it was a tiny footnote in a larger study which ought to have focused on the problems of *conscience* and *casuistry*. I had become sensitive to the fact that it didn't help to try and make sense out of the sorts of developments that I had been concerned with without understanding the structures of conscience and consciousness, and without understanding all of the relations between conscience and the settings and horizons of conscience— the way in which conscience serves as the pivot of a very complex orchestration, a kind of triangulation of institutions, and so on. I saw this and didn't quite know what to do about it. I had already started to work on the other book even before I had finished this one; but I got on to the issue of conscience and casuistry and said to myself, "Well, I'm not really going to try to link up much with the 'cure of souls,' not in the next book, if I ever get it written." But the truth is that I had become interested in the issues of spiritual direction.

As an undergraduate I had become concerned about all of the possible meanings of Freudian theory, especially the theory of symbolism, in reference to cultural expression and productions. Since I am being so autobiographical, I must tell you that my initial efforts in that sphere "turned me off." I found that I could more readily sympathize with the work of D. H. Lawrence and some of his mentors than I could with Karl Abraham, especially with his studies of the area of culture. So I did nothing with it for the longest time—postponed it, so to speak, and said that some day I would get back to the question, "What would a Freudian theory of symbolism have to be in order to throw light upon the sociocultural processes, the actual productions of men in art, in science, in all the spheres of creative activity?"

Now as I worked within this frame of conscience and casuistry I found myself having to hold off this interest in a Freudian theory of symbolism and culture and draw into my interest in "conscience," casuistry and the "cure of souls." Since I didn't really know anything about the evolution of "conscience"—not in any genuine or systematic way—it became imperative to look over that complex of issues very closely. What happened was that I made a certain sort of discovery, familiar enough to theologians who practice it in a forum of conscience, but who, being practitioners, being committed also to many other sorts of interests and obligations, did not perhaps have the opportunity to look at the wider ranges of reference that were embedded in these notions—or at least, so many have told me.

At the risk of overloading the autobiographical content of my argument, I continue:

What I discovered was that the era called the Middle Ages witnessed a flowering—rather than a *nadir*—of the notion of conscience. Feelings of guilt and remorse and conscientiousness had of course existed from time immemorial and are to be found almost everywhere. But I was concerned with making distinctions between behaviorial levels and levels of ordered symbolic articulations—and I have been concerned with this in all the work I have done. I was concerned to analyze the actual logics and dialectics that came to be centered in the notion of "conscience."

I discovered that the concept "conscience" was actually given new thrust in the 11th and 12th centuries. The person who was perhaps most responsible for giving it an extraordinary dimension and range was Abelard. He had most comprehensively articulated the critical questions with respect to intention and had prepared the way for a rethinking of the whole of human activity, despite his own setbacks—for as you know, he was pursued and hunted and hounded for a variety of reasons, including theological ones, by Bernard of Clairvaux, Walter de Saint Thierry and others. It proved to be the case that the entire structure of rationality and thought in the 12th and 13th century was built on the foundations that he had erected. The whole of moral theology and the whole of the canon law had come out of or been reconstituted in the light of the questions that he had asked.

Now, at that time very notable changes were going on in the actual structures of consciousness. (Now I'm speaking with hindsight—I didn't see all of this as I was working). I did recognize that very critical changes were occurring in the structures of consciousness, of which the development of the dialectic and logic of conscience was an absolutely decisive illustration. The great struggles of Bernard of Clairvaux and Abelard needed to be seen in a new light.

If you think about it, there is nothing necessary about the supposition that each of us is possessed of a conscience, which is answerable to whatever, is something that occurred in the course of historic time in response to great complexes of alterations within the texture of relations of man and in the structures of groups and in their perceptions and awarenesses and so on. So there was this notion of "conscience."

Now it proved to be the case that Abelard became a specialist in working out the rationales and problematics, if you will, on the moral conscience. When I say that, I don't mean the remorseful conscience, which only comes into existence *retrospectively*, in the analysis of acts which are known to be sinful or guilty, but the *prospective conscience*. Well, this was a great discovery for me, I must tell you, because I lived in the years when men were "beyond conscience."

There is a book of that title, written some years ago on this campus by Prof. T. V. Smith of the Department of Philosophy. Much of the ethical and political force of the day was really predicated on the supposition that we were *beyond conscience*, that conscience was not really to be taken as a critical component in a logical decision. I think that we all understand this—at least as a basis for my curiosity in that matter. Whenever people thought of conscience, they thought of it as more or less connected to or linked with the *sense of guilt*. Here in the Middle Ages was the supposition of a moral conscience that was *prospective*. In my own experience there were many people who entertained many hopes—political, social—but could not relate very well to the notion of a moral conscience.

So I worked through that and all the problems of the casuistries and discovered that it was an extraordinary kind of relief to discover that at some point or other men had been sufficiently *predicamental* in their vision and had been sufficiently concerned to try to find a place for the activity of conscience in all spheres of existence, that they had in fact elaborated treatises of human acts. They had worked out these *summae* of the cases of conscience and had perceived the necessity of a kind of casuistry of conscience. They kept hammering away at the rationales of conscience; they had also perceived that in the course of our existence all of us at one time or another, in one way or another, fail to keep pace or peace. We go aground and discover that we may need help in one or another way. It seems to me that they had seen this, so that there had actually come into being this extraordinary orchestration and these triangulated institutions of conscience, casuistry and the cure of souls.

I determined to ascertain just what was going on here, to see what was at work, without ever imagining, as I do not imagine now, that I will be truly able to plumb its depth because there are ontological commitments of various sorts which are doubtless caught up here. These would give even greater resonance to the structure than I was actually giving it.

Something which struck me carried me forward here. What if I were to consider all the developments from the Protestant Reformation forward into the 20th century from this perspective? What actually happened when this triangulated structure was broken up for a variety of reasons—which appeared to be very good so far as those who could not tolerate the structure were concerned. They could not tolerate casuistry, since it seemed to them in every case to be a deviation from the moral principle which could be understood with absolute clarity through scripture or through inner light, or through some other source. How was the *casuistry* part of it taken care of? And then, how was the *cure the souls* taken care of? I was keenly interested in that.

So, I worked my way through a great deal of material of the later era, and was, of course, intrigued by how these were taken care of in the 20th century and in the various forms of analysis, particularly Freudian psychoanalysis, and how—if one were to think of all the contemporary forms of therapy and analysis in terms of this complex of functions—these various functions were in fact handled in the framework of the contemporary cure.

Maybe, I thought, I could get a little of this message across to people who were engaged in carrying forward psychoanalysis and psychotherapy in varied shapes and forms, but I failed to do so. The hope that I could was one of the notions that drew me back to the East from the University of Minnesota.

I could not do very much in Minnesota for a variety of reasons. Some of my closest friends among the renowned psychologists and psychoanalysts could not see that these historical matters which were of so much great interest to me might be relevant to them or to their work. They knew the answers to moral questions because in one way or another there was a direct line which gave them the answer that most responsibly, in their view, quickly resolved the moral predicaments. They also felt that there had been developed new thoroughly scientific non-historical ways of relating to the predicaments of men who came into the treatment-situation, a situation which once upon a time was called the *forum of conscience, the cure of souls.*

When I returned East to New York City I thought I could have a greater impact. In a very short time, I was invited to give lectures at psychoanalytic institutes. The first of these were devoted to "symbolism." I temporarily placed my interest in "conscience" between brackets and proceeded to work through the historic unfoldings of structures of existing experiences and expression. Through such an exploration perhaps I could interest practicing therapists in carefully considering all the varied questions which required the articulation of a theory of Symbolism.

This mission failed. Some therapists had some glimmering of what I was talking about. Despite the faintness and implicitness of this knowledge, I managed to find a way to interest some friends in what eventually came to be called objective-relations-analysis—object-relations therapy. This is a very strategic move to make. Allow me to recommend this move to all of you who are interested in carrying forward this kind of work. If we can get psychoanalysts to become interested in object-relations, we can also get them to be interested in the experienced world, to become interested in the predicaments of men in the world, and we can get them to face the complexity of the therapeutic situation in its full range.

What I was trying to do at this level was to work toward a theory of psychoanalytic-psychotherapeutic technique which would describe the situation in terms of what went on in it, of the setting in which it occurred, of all of the ranges of claims that were mediated within the institution, of all the dramatic rehearsals that in fact occurred within the analytic or therapeutic situation, and of all the prospective goals that might be conceivably envisaged as involved in therapy. It is in this context that I welcome the opportunity to rehearse these concerns in this company of students at the University of Chicago, in the presence of Professors Peter Homans and Don Browning who share these concerns.

My message may already be known to many of you, perhaps in a manner that is likely to be more directly effective in whatever work you may propose to do. I did work toward a convincing comprehensive theory of psychoanalytic technique, only to discover to my surprise that few therapists care to concern themeselves with a *theory* of technique. By their own admission, such concern confuses many therapists; therapists want to do treatment and not think about it; indeed, most therapists think it's bad for the doing of it to think about it!

In seeking to strengthen my appeal to therapists, I stressed the fact that initially, at least, it was not necessary for therapists to apply any theory such as mine in the doing of their work; it was enough, if from time to time, they made use of theory in their reflections on what they had done and what had happened in treatment. We do not now have a reliable or comprehensive theory of technique. More critically, we do not have an adequate statement of the analytic situation in several different senses.

Begin at the very heart of the matter. *An individual is under treatment.* Who shall we say he is? And what shall we say are the presenting symptoms? If we advance in our work, we must come to see that the decision as to what these symptoms are is the most critical element in the entire therapeutic relation. We must acknowledge that with the help or hindrance of a particular psychoanalytic theory we can define the situation in such a way as to block access to all of these arenas of experience that are integral to the unfolding of the person in the course of a life in the world. When this happens, our treatment and your image of cure are likely to be flawed.

Now, I went through Freud very carefully from this point-of-view and discovered that at least from my own perspective he had not fulfilled one of his most important promises, which was to produce a theory of psychoanalytic technique. There was a reason for his delay in putting forward a systematic theory of the technique. He had evolved a theory of psychoanalysis which had many different senses for him, one which was to be a kind of foundation for neurology and for the study of psychology generally, but as he worked that out, he built it on certain foundations. Then, as the years passed, his actual clinical experiences were pointing in such other directions that he was unable to pursue right then into their very center. He never did finish writing his work on technique.

A central question that came up in the 1920s is the clue to his unease in regard to these issues. I refer to the debate over the problem of psychosynthesis. A number of theorists and clinicians who were having very great difficulty in their treatment rooms continued to note that it was not inevitably the case that the interpretation of the analyst did put the person together in a way that somehow gave him enhanced agency to act with efficacy and with a certain kind of personhood in respect to the moral, social and other sorts of options that he encountered in his existence. There were analysts who saw that, and who proposed that psychoanalysis did a very great job in some regards. But there was a necessity for another part of treatment called *psychosynthesis*. Freud regarded this as an utterly false idea. He rejected it wholly. Interestingly, his rejection included a revelation of what was a key to something that had hitherto been concealed—not deliberately, by any means—but I suspect concealed from Freud himself. He was committed to a *pre-established harmony*, principally with respect to those components of the complex that had been analyzed out of the complex in the course of the therapeutic situation by the act of interpretation of the analyst. He supposed that when the elements were released from the unhappy complex, they would all find their way back again to a new fusion which would be ego-syntonic as well as world-syntonic; and that the individual would now have new agency, new capacity, enhanced power to function.

Holding the rather restricted view he did, perhaps it is to Freud's credit that he fancied that there were very few moral predicaments in the world, and he thought that almost everyone would know precisely where the moral obligation was. He imagined that the person who had enhanced agency would inevitably want to do what was, in a sense, best for him and for others to do. The issue of synthesis was not for him a central issue, because he so conceived the analytic situation that the job was done when the individual, having worked through the transference-neurosis into which all other neuroses had collapsed, would then work free, and be his own master in a world he was presumably free to make.

Now, I looked at very many other notions, teachings, schools, theories, and points of view. I came to see that I could not, unaided, make very much of an impression on men who were working in this sphere.

Despite all this, I have a continuing conviction that it is of the utmost importance for the comparative, depth-historical study of the social cultural processes, the utmost importance for our understanding of our structures of consciousness as they elaborate across time, the utmost importance for our hopes of being moral agents in very wide senses— that we address ourselves to this whole range of questions that chance to be encapsulated in a form often anachronistic and even repressive—the structure of conscience, casuistry and cure of souls.

To me, it is unthinkable that men should expect to create a new and better world with an ethic that is predicated on a transmoral conscience. It seems imperative that if we are to use the concept or notion of conscience that we shall strive to understand the rationales of conscience and also to apply them to all spheres. It is inconceivable that we should favor conscience without casuistry, which is the situation we have to a very considerable extent today. The fact is that it is precisely now that all of the sorts of issues that are to be disentangled from this complex have an extraordinary kind of importance and urgency.

Recently I have been turning my attention elsewhere. I have become curious about several questions related to my growing interest in the comparative study of civilization and of intercivilizational relations. Does the concept "conscience" give us any clue as to some of the differences in the distinctive patterns of development in various parts of the world? What are the relations between the structures of conscience and the tumultuous sociocultural processes of the 20th century across the world? In brief, I am now persuaded that it is necessary to work one's way back through questions of this sort if we hope to work toward a basic foundation for sociology, history, and psychology and anthropology. We are in great need of a comparative historical analysis of the changing structures of consciousness and conscience across time and places. Some of you may say that we already have such an analysis. We do not. Max Weber did not give it to us; he ran away from questions at that depth. Emile Durkheim had an idea that consciousness and conscience were very decisive spheres to relate to, but he never gave us a comparative historical analysis of the phenomena in this sphere. The fact is that we are now obliged to do a massive amount of work to get anywhere near these questions.

Part II
EAST AND WEST

4. Max Weber, Joseph Needham, Benjamin Nelson: The Question of Chinese Science

N. Sivin

Making the insights of Max Weber and Joseph Needham overlap to illuminate the comparative sociology of science was the last of Benjamin Nelson's many exuberant enthusiasms. When he died unexpectedly in 1977 this great sociologist left a series of essays on what he called civilizational analysis. Four of these publications remarked on the contributions of Joseph Needham as Nelson saw them from a viewpoint nurtured in the traditions of Weber, Durkheim, and Sir Henry Maine.[1] I often found it a source of pleasure and stimulation to hold discourse on Chinese science with Benjamin Nelson, both privately and on several occasions when we shared a podium, over the last five years of his life. I believe that it will be appropriate for me to consider what he had to say, and to suggest some directions in which the inquiry he began might proceed.

The juxtaposition of Weber and Needham is obvious enough on a superficial level. To paraphrase Nelson, they more than any other scholar of this century have revealed on an ample scale the need for, and have shown the way toward, a systematic comparison of civilizations seen as the largest effective units of human thought and action.

On closer examination the similarity is a great deal less obvious, for two reasons that it is difficult to ignore. One is that Weber's concern is capitalism and Needham's is natural science, technology, and mathematics. These interests are, of course, not mutually exclusive, as we would expect of two scholars so motivated by the urgency of present-day dilemmas in which both economic systems and technical activity play such central parts. Weber remarked more than once on science as one of many structures of rationalization. Bourgeois capitalism, as it emerged in the free cities of late medieval Italy, appears to Needham to have been a necessary condition to "bring to fusion point the formerly separated disciplines of mathematics and nature-knowledge." Thus he is convinced that "the failure of the rise of the merchant class to power in the State lies at the basis of the inhibition of the rise of modern science in Chinese society."[2]

Still there can be no doubt that Weber would have found these propositions of Needham's unsatisfactory, as unabashed instances of materialist explanation. Needham is not at all oblivious to non-material factors; in fact he has drawn attention to several that previously had been overlooked. What interests him in the long run, however, is not Weber's interplay of values and social action but the preponderance of one kind of factor over the other: "In sum, I believe that the analysable differences in social and economic pattern between China and Western Europe will in the end illuminate, as far as anything can throw light on it, both the earlier predominance of Chinese science and technology and also the later rise of modern science in Europe alone."[3]

Conversely, Weber's various assertions about Chinese science so inadequately reflect the soundest knowledge readily available about 1910 that he must have been satisfied with casual reading on the topic. Consider this famous passage from *The Religion of China (Konfuzianismus und Taoismus)*:

> The scientific claims of Confucianism were no less modest. The development of mathematics had progressed to trigonometry, but this soon decayed because it was not used. Confucius evidently had no knowledge of the precession of the equinoxes which had been known in the Middle East for a long time. The office of the court astronomer, that is the calendar maker, must be distinguished from the court astrologer who was both an annalist and an influential adviser. The former was a carrier of secret knowledge and his office was hereditarily transmitted. But relevant knowledge can hardly have developed, witness the great success of the Jesuits' European instruments. Natural science as a whole remained purely empirical. Only quotations seem to have been preserved from the old botanical, that is pharmacological work, allegedly the work of an emperor.[4]

Every sentence in this passage is incorrect. Every sentence could have been corrected from sources available ca. 1915.[5]

Needham on capitalism, and Weber on science, did not draw on the best learning within their reach, despite their thoroughness with respect to their own abiding themes.[6] Each found the preoccupation of the other important as an issue, but negligible as an element in research design. The overlap between their arguments and conclusions is thus less than one would expect it to be, given Weber's concern about rationalization and Needham's desire to be precise about the conditions under which modern science emerged.

There is a second reason to retain some doubt about the affinity of Weber and Needham. So far in Needham's books on Chinese science, in 440 pages of index and 911 pages of bibliography, Max Weber does not appear once. This is remarkable considering the pervasiveness of Weber's influence, and Needham's scope of reference. At one point in a discussion of capitalism as a motive force in European history, Needham does suggest that "in the end it will probably be found that all the schools, whether the Weberians, or the Marxists, or the believers in intellectual factors alone, will have their contribution to make."[7] This is hardly an acknowledgement of a major intellectual debt. It is therefore necessary to ask whether in bringing the two together Nelson was not serving as matchmaker for a shotgun wedding.

THE ISSUES

The answer is no. When Nelson repeatedly speaks of "Needham's challenges" he means that, if we consider Weber's intention to account through comparisons for the uniqueness of the European transition to modernity, Needham has demonstrated insufficiencies in Weber's method of approach. He has done so without, as I have said, discussing Weber's work.

Nelson acknowledges several respects in which Needham has carried us further toward sound solutions to the problems Weber has raised. He sees in turn certain limitations in the directions Needham has taken in this effort. These prompt Nelson to turn back to Weber and find in his late writings "clues" which suggest that more adequate replies to "Needham's challenges" may be constructed within the Weberian tradition. To construct them became, in fact, the preoccupation of Nelson's last five years of life. But his final word remained unsaid, and we are left with suggestions.

Needham's Challenge. Nelson identifies Needham's challenge in the form of two propositions. The first is encompassed by the opening paragraphs of *The Grand Titration*: "Apart from the great ideas and systems of the Greeks, between the first and the fifteenth centuries the Chinese, who experienced no 'dark ages,' were generally much in advance of Europe; and not until the scientific revolution of the late Renaissance did Europe draw rapidly ahead. Before that time, however, the West had been profoundly affected not only in its technical processes but in its very social structures and changes by discoveries and inventions emanating from China and East Asia. . . . Why, then, did modern science, as opposed to ancient and medieval science (with all that modern science implied in terms of political dominance), develop only in the Western world?"[8]

Nelson does not accept these claims uncritically; in fact he sees no evidence that Chinese superiority in technology can be extrapolated to what he calls "high-level science."[9] As we will see, he also places the takeoff of Europe long before "the scientific revolution of the Renaissance." Even so, Nelson recognizes the bearing of Needham's larger demonstration on Weber's differential typology. Weber, as Nelson says in another connection, "shied away from dynamic processual analyses of changes . . . in the structures of consciousness." The potentiality that Weber finds unique to the West is unique from the time of the Greeks, at least in germ. What he finds missing in China is missing for the past two thousand years—a period that he does not feel the need to subdivide systematically— and is at best flawed even earlier. Although toward the end of his life Weber became more concerned about "historic rationalizations of science and sensibility," he did not, except by hints, account for the *processes* by which the uniqueness of the West came about.[10] His discussions of change tend to be kinematic, concerned with factors visible in states of society before and after a transition, rather than dynamic, concerned with the ways forces drive events in flux.

Needham is attempting to document Chinese superiority in enterprises that have become the very nucleus of modern civilization. He is suggesting that Europe, rather than being the fated winner in the race to modernity, would have appeared a thousand years ago to be an unlikely contender. The question of Europe's ascendancy cannot be resolved by typology; it is a squarely historical question. That is Needham's first challenge.

For the second challenge Nelson points to a long passage in which Needham states that the Renaissance science that the Jesuits carried to China in the seventeenth century was, unlike the science of an earlier time, no longer "European" or "Western," but rather universal and modern. The missionaries represented it as Western, for they wanted its superiority to be identified as the cultural superiority of Christendom, "but the Chinese understood clearly that it was primarily 'new.' "[11]

Nelson is aware, in citing more recent studies based on the Jesuits' Chinese writings, that the science they were constrained by their church to carry was anything but universal and modern. The Tychonic world system of Tycho Brahe was adopted by the Society of Jesus in the 1620s as part of the Counter-Reformation resistance to cosmological revolution. The physics, geology, meteorology, and other sciences that the missionaries outlined in Chinese were already obsolete in those parts of Europe that were free to choose.[12]

Again a larger point commands attention. In constructing his typologies Weber treats each civilization as a discrete unit, even though he is aware that their borders were permeable and changing. This is perhaps inevitable in view of his concern with ideal types. In any case Needham's emphasis throughout his work, by contrast, is on the ecumenical and world-wide origin of modern science. In his reconstruction of history there is no Western tradition, or Chinese tradition, that can be discussed without reference to impulses passing to and fro across frontiers. Encounters with people, goods, and ideas that have crossed those borders play an essential role in every subdivision of Needham's work. His systematic discourses on the transmission of acupuncture or of conceptions of alchemical immortality are among his most precise and original contributions. The Jesuits' epicycles and tables of logarithms, and Chinese responses to them, constitute merely the last of innumerable encounters that Needham evaluates.

In these encounters Nelson identifies a second challenge. It is a challenge to encompass contacts between civilizations. It draws the attention of Weber's successors to the inevitable press of modern rationalization toward the universal, toward abolishing every local particularity until at the end of the process, if it is ever reached, even the word "civilization" can no longer be used in the plural.

Needham's Contribution. In addition to these critical challenges, the major substantive contribution of Needham to the Weberian enterprise was of course to document the importance of science in shaping the destinies of East and West, and the importance of religion and other cultural factors in shaping the fate of science. This Nelson sees as congruent with Weber's emphasis in his final writings, especially in his introduction to the *Gesammelte Aufsätze zur Religionssoziologie*, on the uniqueness of Western science.[13] Nelson points in his various writings to two other useful insights of Needham.[14] The first is a coupling between mercantile culture and the mathematization of hypotheses, in this assertion from *Science and Civilisation in China:*

> It may well be that concurrent social and economic changes super-
> vening only in Europe formed the milieu in which natural science
> could raise at last above the level of the higher artisanate, the semi-

mathematical technicians. The reduction of all quality to quantities, the affirmation of a mathematical reality behind all appearances, the proclaiming of a space and time uniform throughout all the universe; was it not analogous to the merchant's standard of value? No goods or commodities, no jewels or monies there were, but such as could be computed and exchanged in number, quantity and measure.[15]

Although this turns out to be precisely the causal relationship between capitalism and rationalization that Weber set out to refute, it prompts a stimulating search by Needham for its negative counterpart in China. The second contribution is a contrast between the ideas of law in Europe and China that pointed out the absence in China of a notion of laws of nature, decreed and guaranteed by a divine legislator.[16]

Nelson acknowledges that "Needham is not content to rest his case upon a single or simple formula,"[17] but suggests that his work is vitiated by the tendency to see capitalism as a cause, and the attempt to extrapolate superiority from technology to science, that I have already mentioned. He remarks on Needham's lack of interest in sociological theory, which leads him to overlook such important Weberian themes as the formative character of urban life and the complexity of rationalization as a dynamic force. He also notes that, aside from one or two perceptive passages, Needham overlooks the positive role of religion and theology in the West—the transition in theology and law to new structures of consciousness and a new relation of nature to man, that made the scientific revolution possible later. It is in fact on this ground that Nelson counter-challenges Needham's challenge concerning historical process.

Weber, Nelson reminds us, did not assume that changes in economic and technological priorities will necessarily lead to greater transitions. Modernity is not the result of a linear increase of rationalization, but of successive "charismatic" breakthroughs to new modes of rationalization. Scientific knowledge can arise in any social circumstances; in China it certainly existed, but lacked a metaphysical basis—or so Weber concluded. What prompts change is the "technical utilization" of knowledge, which may be encouraged by capitalism wherever the latter exists, but which becomes possible only in connection with "universalizing and universalistic modes of thought and sensibility." Weber does not ask when these arise, and as a result of what process; Needham does, but his answer, Nelson argues, puts them too late. The crucial period that expanded the possibilities of European science is in the 12th and 13th centuries.[18]

Nelson's own studies in historical sociology led him to believe that in the 12th and 13th centuries Europeans crystallized rationalizing and rationalized structures of consciousness, orientations, and institutions that rest on the "concrete individual person and the objective universal." These structures were the result of efforts in the law and in the universities to institutionalize reason and dialectic, to harmonize these with faith and to produce an "intelligible cosmos . . . and rational world united in all its spheres."[19] The Schoolmen thus maintained a lively interest in Nature; most of the great medieval figures that historians of science study today were theologians by vocation. Their contribution was more than the speculation about impetus, intension and remission of forms, and so on, and the few experiments in magnetism and optics, that Needham has long since acknowledged.[20] It amounts to an institutional framework into which a vastly expanded scientific discourse could fit.

Their stimulus came, of course, from the recovery of Greek and Roman learning. The twelfth and thirteenth centuries were in fact building on "the universalities of Greek philosophy and science, the universalities of Roman law and political theory." The evolution of modern science, for Nelson as for Weber, is traced in the vicissitudes of the Greek heritage. Without its influence, they are convinced, no universally valid scientific knowledge, backed by a vivifying metaphysics, has ever existed. The twelfth and thirteenth centuries represent, in Nelson's view, a unique discontinuity in the history of this legacy. In the "fraternizing" atmosphere of medieval cities it was combined once and for all with Christianity's universalization of human brotherhood. The result was a setting for widening exploratory debates that have continued to the present.[21]

Further Challenges

That was how far Nelson was able to carry his response to Needham's challenges. There is no doubt that, given more time, he would have dealt substantively with the issue of encounters between civilizations, and would have further developed the arguments that I have just summarized through his growing acquaintance with Chinese science. Let me finally suggest how they might be further developed.

The Scientific Revolution Problem. For Weber comparative studies were necessary to explain the uniqueness of Western institutions. They made possible a typology of the reciprocal relations between ideas and social possibilities. Even more fundamental, one must first know what is missing elsewhere if one is to make what Weber called "a clearer genetic comparison of the historical uniqueness of European cultural development."[22] It is not that Europe furnishes the only development worth studying for its own sake, but that Weber's concern is to create "an empirical science of concrete reality" (*Wirklichkeitswissenschaft*). His aim, he goes on to say, "is that understanding of the characteristic uniqueness of the reality *in which we move.*" This is neither cultural bias nor pretended disinterestedness, but rather a commitment to the affairs of his own time.[23] It gives the historical realities of Europe a poignancy by contrast to which Weber sees Chinese civilization as exotic.

This enduring focus on Europe needs to be kept in mind as we contemplate Weber's interest in why capitalism did not develop autochthonously in China, and as we consider alongside it Needham's contagious curiosity about why modern science did not first appear in China. It has seldom been noticed how inherently problematic these queries are. They are examples of a type of question that has not been asked in science since the time of Leibniz, and that fastidious historians in this century have tended to avoid and to teach their students to avoid. Why does a body not fall with a speed proportional to the cube of the elapsed time? Why is France not a socialist state? Why was your automobile not stolen from the curb last night as you were sleeping? These translate into questions about what actually is the case. They can only be answered by an account of what did happen. Such questions continue to be asked, of course, because of their heuristic value. They arouse interest in a topic and provide some initial order for thinking about it. As we comprehend it better they tend to grow murky. Finally they lose their interest compared with the emerging clarity of what did happen.

Although the aims of Weber and Needham clearly are heuristic, their particular questions remain problematic. On what ground can we assume that people in other civilizations wanted or were unconsciously working toward economic systems or scientific theories of a modern type? If they were not, on what ground can we speak of their values or institutions "handicapping" or "hindering" these developments, as Weber does,[24] or "inhibiting" them, as Needham and writers inspired by him do?

Sociological Perspectives. One of the most impressive results of juxtaposing the writings of Weber and Needham, both of them scholars committed to social frames of reference, is to see how relentlessly unsociological they are when they consider China. I presume that sociology, even of the sort most purely devoted to cognition, is concerned with what identifiable collectivities share. These collectivities need not be united in space or time, but their membership must be definable. The study of a disembodied idea extant only in an ancient classic may belong to either philosophy or intellectual history, but can be considered sociological only if sooner or later the idea takes on a special meaning for an identifiable collectivity.

By the first century B. C. the central notions of the Analects, the *Lao-tzu,* and so on, had become the common property of Chinese culture. I need not repeat my detailed arguments about the confusions that have sprung from Sinologists' consistently ambiguous use of the words "Confucianism" and "Taoism."[25] The consequences of this ambiguity are visible in Weber's writing, as they are in Needham's. Weber's tendencies to reify "Confucianism" so that it becomes the subject of active verbs, and to treat it as shorthand for "dominant social and political forces" of many kinds were characteristic of Sinological usage at the time he wrote.

We have made a little progress in recent decades. More precision of the same kind, applied to the relations between values and social change, can further strengthen Weber's heritage.

Our understanding of science as a class of rationalizations in China can also benefit from concern with who was doing it. Most writing on social aspects of Chinese science and technology has been concerned with individuals, with abstract sets such as all those who would agree with some sentiment of Lao-tzu or Chuang-tzu, or with members of socio-economic classes.[26] More attention might be given to lineages (which in science as in religion are determined by the transmission of a charismatic text) and to the few coherent occupational groups that can be identified, such as court astronomers and physicians. Attention of this sort has recently led to several findings that change the conventional picture of Chinese science:

1. There was no science in traditional China, only sciences. Contrary to the picture that Weber drew from his sources, these were sophisticated enough that we can evaluate them on the same level as their contemporary European counterparts until the seventeenth century. Which were better and which worse remains a matter of opinion. But they were not integrated by anything corresponding to the *scientia* of the West. *Scientia* was, after all, born and maintained in social institutions, from the Academy and Lyceum to the medieval universities, that subordinated science to philosophy. This was not the case in China.[27]

2. As we might suspect from the first point, the advancement of science in China cannot be attributed to Taoists by any socially meaningful definition of the latter word. Alchemy is the only science particularly associated with Taoist sects. What chemical processes and what chemical knowledge originated in alchemy, and what was borrowed from medicine and the chemical arts to be applied toward macrobiotic and meditational ends? That question remains entirely open. Conversely, in the sciences generally, most famous contributions were made by conventional people who followed civil service careers. In technology they were made by craftsmen whose religious affiliations on the whole remain unknown.

3. Theoretical scientific endeavors existed in China, and customarily overlapped those aimed toward practical goals. Recognition that this was

the case has been much delayed by the failure of Sinologists to study systematically theoretical and metaphysical writings, on the ground that any discourse about yin-yang and the Five Phases must be gobbledygook or flim-flam. Incompetent translations of medical writings have merely reinforced this conviction. But like other Chinese documents, those of theoretical science yield to the scholarship that Giorgio de Santillana defined as "the art of reading slowly."[28]

From these writings emerges a conviction that bears on any sociology of cognition. Their authors did not believe that empirical investigation integrated by theory could completely explain physical phenomena. It could yield useful answers to any practical question, but the texture of reality is too fine and too subtle to be completely apprehended by extending the senses. For access to the inwardness of Nature, means are readily at hand, namely introspection, contemplation, or a leap of intuition, depending on the teaching of various traditions. These means are complementary to those of science, a point that affects both.[29]

The Marginality of Revolutionary Change. My final point is a corollary of the preceding one. If we consider the process that underlies Weber's leap from tradition to modernity, we notice that he is studying a group of European sects that we see emerging from the margins of society to change the world around them, or disappear, or both. It is precisely their marginality—and a transitional situation that furnishes them with openings to a mutable center—that lets them be revolutionary. In this focus on the edges of society Weber differs crucially from Nelson, whose schoolmen of the twelfth and thirteenth centuries become the intellectual establishment of Catholic Europe soon after they appear.

When Weber's gaze shifts to China it quickly becomes fixed on the elite and its literary heritage, both what it drew from Confucius and what it drew from Lao-tzu. His Confucians and Taoists, like Needham's, are too often the same people. Occasionally Weber glances toward the outer reaches of society—with his tendency to see the last two thousand years in one featureless blur—but his eyes are soon forced back by a prospect of irrationality and unredeemed traditionalism that only the shock of Westernization could possibly break through. Here again we see Weber's sound instincts thwarted by the limitations of his sources. A great deal is explained by his statement that "the sociologist essentially depends on the literature of missionaries. This certainly varies in value but in the last analysis remains relatively the most authentic."[30]

The issue of marginality turns out to be equally important with respect to scientific revolutions. That is perhaps the most important conclusion that we can readily draw in connection with Needham's second challenge, in which the Jesuits typify the encounter between civilizations. Indian astronomers in the eighth century; Islamic astronomers from Central Asia in the thirteenth century; Christian missionaries around 1600: all brought versions of Ptolemaic astronomy and Aristotelian cosmology that could have precipitated revolutionary changes. The Jesuits did so, but only in astronomy, not in society. Their teaching was confined to the elite, to people whose first thought was for the preservation and revivification of their own culture. If we seek in China those for whom science was not a means to conservative ends, for whom one proven fact could in principle outweigh the whole body of millennial values, we do not find them until the late nineteenth century. By that time foreigners exempt from Chinese law and backed by gunboats had educated them and given them prospects of careers. We can no longer talk about the encounter of the old and new astronomy. Social and political change had left nothing for the old to do. Chinese astronomy was no longer taught.

CONCLUSION

These reflections suggest that Needham's challenges remain on the whole intact. In identifying them Benjamin Nelson made a most important contribution to the sociology that builds on Weber's avoidance of reductionism. Nelson's answer to the first challenge, the challenge to explain process, carried our attention back to the notion of *scientia* that began to evolve in European circumstances as soon as the stimulus of Islamic classicism was felt in the twelfth and thirteenth centuries. It did not come to grips with Needham's important point that by 1635 the Schoolmen had come to constitute a disciplined opposition to emerging modern science. In this transition lies a most fundamental question of social process. Let those who must now face this question remember the ebullient and tenacious man whose explorations have led them to see the issues in that way.

NOTES

1. "Civilizational Complexes and Intercivilizational Encounters," *Sociological Analysis* 34 (1973):79–105. "Weber's Protestant Ethic: Its Origins, Wanderings, and Foreseeable Futures," in *Beyond the Classics? Essays in the Scientific Study of Religion,* ed. by Charles T. Glock and Phillip E. Hammond (New York: Harper Torchbooks, 1973). "On the Shoulders

of the Giants of the Comparative Historical Sociology of 'Science'—in Civilizational Perspective," in, *Social Processes of Scientific Development*, ed. by R. D. Whitley (London, 1974). "Sciences and Civilizations, 'East' and 'West.' Joseph Needham and Max Weber," *Boston Studies in the Philosophy of Science* 11 (1974):445–493.

2. Joseph Needham, *Science and Civilisation in China* (Cambridge, England: Cambridge University Press, 1954-), III, pp. 150–168, esp. p. 168.; *The Grand Titration: Science and Society in East and West* (London: Allen & Unwin, 1969), p. 186.

3. Joseph Needham, *The Grand Titration*, p. 217.

4. Max Weber, *The Religion of China: Confucianism and Taoism*, ed. and tr. by Hans H. Gerth (New York: Free Press, 1964), p. 154.

5. The more extended passage on pp. 196–198 under the heading *"The Systematic Rationalization of Magic"* is no better. The problem was not one of accessibility, but was rather due to Weber's preference for the writings of Protestant over Catholic missionaries. To give a single example, the extensive writings of the Jesuit Antoine Gaubil on the history of Chinese astronomy in *Observations mathématiques, astronomiques, géographiques, chronologiques et physiques tirées des anciens livres chinois ou faites nouvellement aux Indes et à la Chine, et ailleurs, par les Pères de la Compagnie de Jésus*, ed. by E. Souciet, 2 vols. (Paris, 1729–1732), and in *Letters édifiantes et curieuses, écrites des Missions Etrangères*, XXVI (Paris, 1783), pp. 65–295, are far from superseded in any Western language even today.

6. The last word from Needham, of course, has still to be heard. His full discussion of the role of capitalism and other factors in China's early technical development is to appear in Vol. VII of *Science and Civilisation in China*. But there are no indications so far that he will be drawing on the Weberian tradition and on more recent approaches in historical sociology.

7. Joseph Needham, *The Grand Titration*, p. 40.

8. Benjamin Nelson, "Sciences and Civilizations," pp. 449–451. Joseph Needham, *The Grand Titration*, p. 11.

9. Nor do I. If the comparison is between the uninterrupted scientific traditions of China and the detritus that survived the debacle of classical culture in Western Europe, it ignores the achievements of Greek science, which remained influential outside Europe and were crucial to the medieval revival. Needham adduces the Graeco-Roman heritage in "The Roles of Europe and China in the Evolution of Oecumenical Science," *Advancement of Science* 24 (1967):83–98. He argues elsewhere that despite the superiority of Greek theoretical rigor and predictive techniques to those of China a thousand years later, Chinese made estimable contributions to cosmology, instrumentation, and observational records; see *Sciences and Civilisation in China*, III, pp. 458–460. One can hardly conclude from Needham's argument that Chinese astronomy was therefore on balance "much in advance of its Western counterpart." In this concrete passage Needham makes no such claim; he merely asserts that the Chinese tradition "requires a much more important place in the history of science as a whole than historians have been wont to give it." I would say no more than that for the other Chinese sciences.

10. Benjamin Nelson, "Civilizational Complexes," pp. 84–86; 88–90. Nelson, "Max Weber's 'Author's Introduction'; (1920): A Master Clue to his Main Aims," *Sociological Inquiry* 44 (1974):269–278.

11. Needham, *Science and Civilisation in China*, III, pp. 448–449.

12. N. Sivin, "Copernicus in China," *Studia Copernicana* 6 (1973):63–122. Willard J. Peterson, "Western Natural Philosophy Published in Late Ming China," *Proceedings of the American Philosophical Society* 17 (1973):295–322.

13. B. Nelson, "Sciences and Civilizations," pp. 446; "Weber's 'Author's Introduction,' " p. 273.

14. Nelson, "Sciences and Civilizations," pp. 453–457; "Civilizational Complexes," p. 86.

15. Needham, *Science and Civilisation in China*, III, p. 166.

16. Needham, *Science and Civilisation in China*, II, pp. 518–583. Derk Bodde has taken issue with this position in "Evidence for 'Laws of Nature' in Chinese Thought," *Harvard Journal of Asiatic Studies* 20 (1957):709–727, and "Chinese 'Laws of Nature': A Reconsideration," 39 *ibid.* (1979):139–155. Bodde has argued that there was "a minority viewpoint . . . which was a good deal more congenial to the ideas underlying the 'laws of nature' than would at first sight be expected." There remains an objection even more to the point: no one has demonstrated that belief in a supreme being who created the universe and laid down its laws, a belief which according to Needham underlies the notion of laws of nature, is a necessary condition for science of the modern type. One might argue to the contrary that a conception of natural order as in some sense legislated has ceased for some time to play an integral part in the evolution of modern science. If it is not a necessary condition, I fail to comprehend why its absence in China has any explanatory value. The cogency of the comparison seems, in fact, to be seriously undermined by lack of clear evidence that any term corresponding to "law of nature" played a role in classical philosophy. It was the Jewish thinker Philo of Alexandria in the first century A.D. who first "liberally employed" the term *nomos physeos* in this sense. Earlier, as Needham says, we find conceptions of homeostasis as justice and of human law based in part on this cosmic order; but these principles are not thought of as established by a divine lawgiver. See Helmut Koester, "NOMOS PHYSEOS. The Concept of Natural Law in Greek Thought," in, *Religions in Antiquity: Essays in Memory of Erwin Ramsdell Goodenough*, ed. by Jacob Neusner (Leiden: Studies in the History of Religions, Supplements to *Numen* 14, 1968), pp. 521–541. For further exploration of problematic aspects of Needham's work see the systematic analysis in Sal P. Restivo, "Joseph Needham and the Comparative Sociology of Chinese and Modern Science," *Research in Sociology of Knowledge, Sciences and Art* 2 (1979):25–51.

17. Nelson, "Sciences and Civilizations," p. 451.

18. Nelson, "Sciences and Civilizations," pp. 472, 463, *et passim*.

19. Nelson, "Sciences and Civilizations," p. 473.

20. Needham, *Science and Civilisation in China*, III, pp. 161–162.

21. Nelson, "Sciences and Civilizations," pp. 467, 473. There is no need for the present purpose to evaluate Nelson's criticisms of Needham one by one. See the Conclusion of this essay.

22. Nelson, "Weber's 'Author's Introduction,' " p. 273.

23. Max Weber, *Max Weber on the Methodology of the Social Sciences* (Glencoe, IL: Free Press, 1949), p. 72.

24. Max Weber, *The Religion of China*, p. 104.

25. N. Sivin, "On the Word 'Taoist' As a Source of perplexity. With Special Reference to the Relations of Science and Religion in Traditional China," *History of Religions* 17 (1978):303–330.

26. In *The Refiner's Fire, The Enigma of Alchemy in East and West* (J. D. Bernal Lecture, Birkbeck College, London, 1971), pp. 15 and 30, Needham takes exception to "the usual unawareness of the explanatory power of sociological distinctions," but his own discussion refers only to the "radical difference of social class between the artisan metal-workers and the dilettante philosophers."

27. See for instance N. Sivin, ed., *Science and Technology in East Asia* (New York: History of Science, Selections from *Isis*, 1977), p. xvi.

28. A model of philological analysis, restricted to a textual tradition within medicine, is Manfred Porkert, *The Theoretical Foundations of Chinese Medicine* (Cambridge, MA: MIT East Asian Science Series, 3, 1974). I have examined closely the use of theoretical concepts in alchemy in Needham, *Science and Civilisation in China*, V.4, pp. 210–305.

29. N. Sivin, "Shen Kua," *Dictionary of Scientific Biography* XII (1975):369–393, esp. 385–387.

30. Max Weber, *The Religion of China*, p. 231.

5. Nature on Trial:
The Case of the Rooster That Laid an Egg

E. V. Walter

In 1474, a chicken passing for a rooster laid an egg, and was prosecuted by law in the city of Basel. Now, we are inclined to dismiss the event as fowl play, but in those days *lusus naturae* was no joke. The animal was sentenced in a solemn judicial proceeding and condemned to be burned alive "for the heinous and unnatural crime of laying an egg." The execution took place "with as great solemnity as would have been observed in consigning a heretic to the flames, and was witnessed by an immense crowd of townsmen and peasants."[1] The same kind of prosecution took place in Switzerland again as late as 1730.

In the case of the Rooster of Basel, the executioner found three more eggs in him, according to a chronicle of the city. A recent historian, E. P. Evans, reporting the case, refused to believe that part of the chronicle, declaring it absurd, and regarding the event "not [as] a freak of nature, but [as] the freak of an excited imagination tainted with superstition."[2] Evans knew that eggs presumed to come out of roosters caused panic because people used to believe that cocks' eggs were used in witchcraft. Moreover, the same egg, according to an ancient folk belief, might produce a dreaded monster known as the basilisk or cockatrice, a malignant, winged reptile with the head of a cock and the tail of a serpent, which destroyed men and things by its breath and its glance.[3] Regarding the superstition as absurd, Evans considered it equally absurd to expect eggs from roosters. Like most of us, he assumed that any egg under suspicion could ultimately be traced to a hen.

Yet, neither the history of poultry nor the intimate record of the barnyard will support the dogmatism of Evans. In the winter of 1921–22, the *National Poultry Journal* of London was full of news about a chicken being exhibited in a poultry show at Westminster, which attracted a great deal of interest. A Buff Orphington with the voice and manners of a hen but with the plumage of a rooster, it was reported to have laid eggs. The truth was obscured because a practical joker kept putting all kinds of eggs of different colors from different breeds into the pen. But a student at the Eyresford Training Centre, overcome by the zeal to know the truth, performed a crucial experiment, which has almost been lost to history. In the January 6, 1922 issue of the *National Poultry Journal*, Mr. H. M. B. Spurr reported his observations. On December 22, a fellow trainee had noticed that the bird in question had laid an egg. On the 24th, Mr. Spurr, who was on trapnesting duty, found the bird in No. 4 nest box, No. 6 pen, at 11:45 a.m. He immediately took possession of the poultry house key, locked the house, and continued this tour of duty. Returning at 12:25, he released the bird, and removed a small but typical Buff Orphington egg. In his own words, as reported in the *National Poultry Journal* of Great Britain, "Seeing is believing, Sir, and although previously doubtful I am now assured . . . that this 'cock of the south' does not lie—it lays."[4]

On this side of the Atlantic, the case of the Rooster of Madison was reported in the *Journal of Heredity* in 1927. The bird had the plumage of a Brown Leghorn cock, but was laying eggs, and was acquired as a curiosity by the Poultry Husbandry Department of the Wisconsin Experiment Station in 1922, the same year that the Buff Orphington was attracting attention in England. To a casual observer, the Wisconsin bird had the full plumage of a rooster, but anyone intimate with poultry would have recognized that the head and body of the bird were rather effeminate. In order to settle the question of egg production conclusively, the bird was put into a padlocked wire cage, with a screen that would not allow eggs to be sneaked into it, in a closed room. An unlaid egg in the oviduct had already been detected, and the following morning, a normal Brown Leghorn egg was found in the cage. Following that, the alleged rooster laid eggs about every other day.[5]

L. J. Cole, a geneticist at the University of Wisconsin, published a picture of the Rooster of Madison, taken on February 17, 1922, together with three of its eggs, arranged from left to right in the order they were laid on February 13, 15, and 17 respectively. Cole concluded that if Evans, writing in 1906, could have seen this picture, he would not have been so ready to doubt the chronicle telling that the executioner cut open the Rooster of Basel in 1474 and "found three more eggs in him." The Rooster of Madison continued to lay regularly over a long period of time.[6]

An explanation may be found in the dynamics of sex expression in poultry. Under certain conditions, a fowl may take on secondary sex characteristics that contradict its reproductive anatomy. Farmers know that sometimes hens exhibit male plumage and other masculine attributes, and studies have shown that this condition is associated invariably with tumors or some other diseased condition of the ovary. If the ovary is removed, a hen grows male feathers, and the changes that accompany progressive ovarian tumors resemble the sequellae of ovariotomy. Some hens may experience a temporary disturbance of the ovarian function and grow male plumage, but as the ovary returns to normal, they continue to lay eggs. Meanwhile, the bird's dress will be out of harmony with its physiology, and it must wait until the next molt before it looks like a hen once more.

The alleged Rooster of Madison in the spring of 1922 did not fool a certain White Leghorn male. She was mated with that authentic rooster, behaving, in spite of her appearance, like a normal female, and lived happily ever after. The eggs hatched out of that union produced chicks that grew into ordinary barnyard citizens and lived uneventful lives. She recovered the normal plumage of a female in the fall molt of 1922, returned to the existence of an ordinary hen, and disappeared from history.[7]

Cole suggested that such a return to normal, while probably less common than a progressive course of ovarian disease, happened often enough to explain the references to "cocks' eggs" in ancient and medieval times. Contrary to Evans's assumption that the Rooster of Basel was framed, and that the eggs were really produced by some other bird, Cole believed that the accused bird had actually laid those eggs. He concluded that "its guilt lay in looking like a cock when it was in reality a hen."[8]

Let us examine comparatively the social impact of alleged roosters who have thrust upon them the reputation of laying eggs. The Rooster of Madison provokes little more than a chuckle—perhaps appearing as a curiosity in the pages of a newspaper, if the events were to happen today, or possibly inspiring a notice in Ripley's *Believe It Or Not*. A mechanistic explanation drawn from biology calms any disturbance we might feel. In contrast, the Rooster of Basel in the 15th century had gathered an enormous crowd and had generated a wave of fear and excitement. But in traditional China, Joseph Needham tells us, when an apparent rooster laid an egg, the chicken would go unharmed, but the provincial governor or even the emperor might be in serious trouble. He could be impeached and removed from office,[9] for such a rare and frightening event would be regarded as a reprimand from Heaven. Although one finds numerous accounts of sex reversal in man and animals in Chinese literature, and even enlightened discussions of the phenomena, these occurrences remained prodigies. Seers and diviners pondered their implications for the future and for the affairs of state.[10] Nature and society were expected to remain in a condition of organic harmony, and if the harmony were disturbed by the appearance of biological anomalies, it was often assumed that the emperor or some other great official was at fault. Needham argues that animal trials were unthinkable in China because the Chinese were never so presumptuous as to pretend to know what God had in mind for delinquent roosters. Besides, the notion of the law of nature as a command that should be enforced was alien to the Chinese.

In Western civilization, Needham reminds us, the laws of nature, in a scientific sense, and natural law, in a juristic sense, shared a common root,[11] which had coercive implications. Things and animals and people were commanded to behave according to the rules given by the transcendent legislator, subject to divine sanctions. The Chinese sense of natural order, in contrast, depended on an idea of inevitable cooperation. In Needham's words, "The harmonious cooperation of all beings arose, not from the orders of a superior authority external to themselves, but from the fact that they were all parts in a hierarchy of wholes forming a cosmic pattern, and what they obeyed were the internal dictates of their own natures."[12]

Laws of nature, in the Western sense, Needham suggests, may have reached the limits of usefulness. Western science is abandoning mechanical causation for organic causality in a "great movement of our time towards a rectification of the mechanical Newtonian universe by a better understanding of the meaning of natural organisation."[13] Modern science is being obliged "to incorporate into its own structure" an organic view of the world that is typically Chinese.[14] Yet, Needham suspects that the old Western view of natural law may have been an essential phase in the rise of modern science. He wonders if "the recognition of . . . statistical regularities and their mathematical expression could have been reached by any other road than that which Western science actually travelled." He concludes with an intriguing question: "Was perhaps the state of mind in which an egg-laying cock could be prosecuted at law necessary in a culture which should later have the property of producing a Kepler?"

I intend to take the question seriously and explore the road that led from the Rooster of Basel to Kepler. It is my way of responding to what Benjamin Nelson called "Needham's Challenge." This program of inquiry seeks to explain, by comparative method, and by differentiating and clarifying specific factors, why modern science developed originally in Western Europe and nowhere else. My own inquiry takes a different turn and searches for the occasions that led up to the spiritual revolution that produced not only modern science, but also what Weber called "the disenchantment of the world." On the way, I have turned up what I believe are some modest clues to the great question posed by Needham's

Challenge as well. Needham tells us, "historically the question remains whether natural science could ever have reached its present state of development without passing through a 'theological' stage."[16] In this paper I have enlarged that observation to understand that the word "theological" includes the term "demonological" as well. I shall go so far as to propose that demonology is a link that fastens, a hyphen that binds the idea of law to the idea of nature, at least until the end of the 17th century.

Because Needham's attention remains with the rational side of natural law, he prefers to neglect the demonic side. But in the minds of the people who executed them, egg-laying cocks were no ordinary lawbreakers. They inspired sacred dread, for they were possessed by evil spirits, their eggs might be used in witchcraft, or they might hatch preternatural monsters. Their moral and religious relationship to the demonic world obliged Christians to try those chickens and execute them. Chinese also believed in demons and bad spirits, but their system of belief differed in crucial ways. Unlike them, Western Christians were urged by a moral imperative to scrutinize nature and to put unusual phenomena on trial.

Until the modern world view made its familiar impact, all the great civilizations experienced nature through a system of perceptions and ideas that is usually called "animism." In this mode of experience, nature was full of spirits, and natural objects endowed with a living principle that also vitalized the human soul. In the most familiar varieties of animism, nature was a society of souls, often including minerals, plants, animals, and humans. The forces of nature, therefore, were understood as personal forces, and spirits held personally responsible for causing natural phenomena and their good or evil consequences. It does not matter if Durkheim is right and totemism was older than animism. Nor does it matter if Marett is right and animism was preceded by "pre-animism." For our purposes, it is enough to recognize that animism was widespread and, one is tempted to say, universal. However, it is also important to recognize that animistic systems differed from one another in important ways, and that these differences had consequences.

Nineteenth-century writers liked to associate animism with primitivity, but that connection loses its meaning if we recognize the varieties of Greek, Roman, Buddhist, Chinese, Christian, Egyptian, Hebrew, Indian, Japanese, Muslim, and Persian animism. The Hastings *Encyclopedia of Religion and Ethics* describes twenty demonological systems, setting "civilized" cheek by jowl with "primitive" forms. Previously, comparative inquiries have tended to stress the common features of animistic thinking. Now I am suggesting that we look at them differentially, and I shall argue that the peculiar features that distinguish Occidental Christian animism from other systems may have an important bearing on Needham's question about the emergence of modern science in the West.

The history of science is the history of human relationships with nature. Werner Heisenberg writes that "science is but a link in the infinite chain of man's argument with nature," and science "cannot simply speak of nature 'in itself'."[17] He insists, "When we speak of the picture of nature in the exact science of our age, we do not mean a picture of nature so much as a *picture of our relationships with nature.* . . . Science, we find, is now focused on the network of relationships between man and nature, on the framework which makes us as living beings dependent parts of nature, and which we as human beings have simultaneously made the object of our thoughts and actions. Science no longer confronts nature as an objective observer, but sees itself as an actor in this interplay between man and nature."[18] Animistic thinking understood the interplay as a set of moral relationships. As the American Indian writer, Vine DeLoria, observes, when the white man wants to stop polluting the river, he does not stop thinking of the river as a mechanism. In contrast, the traditional Indian asks about his responsibility to the river as a living being. The modern European assumes that moral ideas are not relevant to the workings of inanimate things. He has drawn a boundary and placed the river on the other side of it. The history of the boundary settlement underlying such European assumptions is the subject of this paper. It is the history of the great transition from animism to mechanism.

In every human society, people believe that some unobservable order, personal or impersonal, includes causes and reasons that transcend and explain the phenomena of experience. Nathan Sivin has observed that even though the idea of the Unseen Order does not fit the standard categories of intellectual history, it is one of the greatest of man's imaginative conceptions. As William James observed, "Such is the human ontological imagination, and such is the convincingness of what brings it to birth. Unpicturable beings are realized, and realized with an intensity almost like that of an hallucination. . . . They are as convincing to those who have them as any direct sensible experiences can be, and they are, as a rule, much more convincing than results established by mere logic ever are."[19]

The Unseen Order in traditional China was understood by impersonal, abstract concepts, such as *yang* and *yin* and the five elements. It was also filled with personal spirits: ghosts, demons, gods, and so forth. In the world of Chinese medicine, Sivin has shown us, the impersonal abstract concepts belonged to the "great tradition" of China's tiny educated elite.But for vitality, it depended on the "small tradition" of the common folk, "whose world was not only much more intellectually restricted but full of personal forces, spirits and ghosts, which brought and took away sickness and other visitations of fate. . ." Although the two realms enjoyed a symbiotic relationship, it was always possible, over centuries, to discern the border between "the spiritualistic world view of folk medicine and the abstract speculative cosmology of classical medicine. . . ."[20]

In the Chinese scheme, the boundaries between ghosts, demons, and gods were fluid, and a single spirit might become all three. The Occidental scheme maintained rigid boundaries, and ghosts, demons, and gods always had distinct indentities and did not cross class lines. Another difference was the presence or absence of moral segregation. Max Weber pointed out that the Chinese demonology lacked a principle of radical evil, and that spirits would commit good or evil deeds depending on their circumstances. Both Confucianism and Taoism, the major forms of religious expression in China, "lacked even traces of a satanic force of evil against which the pious Chinese, whether orthodox or heterodox, might have struggled for his salvation."[21] In contrast, the Occidental demonology segregated the invisible world into realms of good and evil spirits. Christian dualistic animism imposed certain obligations on religious communities. One of these obligations was to stand guard in the realm of nature, ready to place natural phenomena on trial, testing them for good and evil. From the middle of the 14th century until the 18th century, Europeans tried to control the demonic forces in nature by trials for witchcraft. As Lea wrote, "All destructive elemental disturbances—droughts or flood, tempests or hail-storms, famine or pestilence—were ascribed to witchcraft."[22]

For religious reasons, then, European Christians were obliged to carry out experiments. They could not leave nature alone. These experiments, we shall see, were carried out not in laboratories, but in the courts. Christian dualistic animism inspired a conspiratorial view of the universe, leaving men confronted with the terrors of a vast spiritual underworld bent on ruining them for eternity. The church assumed the responsibility of exorcising the Devil in all his manifestations. It was the province of the courts to cooperate in this spiritual police action against *maleficia*, or evil magical actions, against diabolic agencies, malicious spirits, watchful fiends, and crowds of demons. Both church and judiciary expressed a horror of collaboration with evil spirits, trying to limit the power of demons over mankind by catching their agents *in flagrante delictu*. As Langton observes, "The belief in demons and the belief in witches are but two aspects of the same belief; for the witch is a person through whom the demon chooses to manifest itself."[23] Studies in comparative demonology will reveal no other animistic system in which law and judicial proceedings play such an important part. Like the trials for witchcraft, animal trials illustrate the unique and peculiar legalism of Occidental demonology.

Lynn White has shown the importance of the moral and "emotional basis for the objective investigation of nature" in the later Middle Ages.[24] He has also observed that modern science, emerging in that period, "was more than the product of a technological impulse: it was one result of a deep-seated mutation in the general attitude towards nature, of the change from a symbiotic-subjective to a naturalistic-objective view of the physical environment."[25] Although scientific thought developed apart from the courtroom, the changing moral and emotional relation to nature may be traced in the trials that tested the presence or absence of demons in the behavior of animals as well as humans.

The moral imagination of the West is juridical, and the courts have remained near the center of moral and spiritual life, and never remote from the vital currents of intellectual concern. For centuries, courtroom debates enlarged or defined the boundaries of scientific as well as theological issues. As Coulton observed, "just as legal theories crept into medieval demonology, so did demonology creep into the law-courts."[26] The legalistic demonology of the West made the Christian form of dualistic animism different from any other kind.

Before disenchantment, the natural world was not differentiated from the world, and the world was experienced and understood through categories that were not only moral but also theological and demonological. God may have "owned" the world, but the Devil "possessed" it, or at least a good part of it. For the early Christians, the Devil was the prince of this world. However, they also believed, as the Vulgate tells us, that ". . . princeps huius mundi iam iudicatus est" (John 16:11): the prince of this world has already been judged. The case was closed, but, as Tertullian put it in his Apologia, written around the beginning of the 3rd century, even though the evil demons had been condemned, it gave them some comfort before their ultimate punishment to act out their malignant dispositions. According to Tertullian, "Their great business is the ruin of mankind" (Apol. 22, 26). Sermons, tales, and other pious writings shaped a collective experience of the world that personified danger and evil. Through this literature, people learned to ascribe an uncanny or unusual experience to the Devil. As a medieval historian put it, the Devil "inspires evil thoughts, instigates crimes, and causes any unhappy or immoral happening. It is just as much a matter of course as if one should say to-day, I have a cold, or John stole a ring, or James misbehaved with So-and-So."[27]

The world was an arena in which God and the Devil made competing claims on human loyalty. Men and women who chose to ally themselves with the Devil were guilty of spiritual treason. That is why witches in the

15th and 16th centuries drew such heavy retribution. In giving aid and comfort to the Eternal Enemy, they had committed high treason or *lèse majesté* against God.

Christian speculation about the world developed a legalistic theory about the relation between God and Satan. The world, lost through sin, had become the Devil's property through right of possession. In order to remain just, God would not injure the Devil or remove him by force. The world must be ransomed by something more valuable than the world, and God exchanged his Son for the world.Christ's death, therefore, bought Humanity back from Satan. Roman thought tended to legal formulations, and this theory, which began in the East, took hold in the West. "The Western church, therefore, took kindly to that view of the Atonement which represented it as the result of a lawsuit between God and the Devil."[28] Medieval writers described imaginary dialogues in a cosmic courtroom between God and the Devil. In some of them, God and the Devil divided the real estate of the world. Usually, the Devil claimed the largest expanses, but those turned out to be deserts and arid mountain tops.[29] That helped to explain why deserts and wild places were haunted by demons. Sometimes, the Devil went to court to defend his demons, witches, and other associates. Pierre de Lancre, a distinguished magistrate of Bordeaux, who investigated sorcery allegations in the Basque region, wrote a book in 1611. It included an anecdote about a Witch's Sabbath. The Devil had missed several previous Sabbaths, and when he finally reappeared, the witches and warlocks greeted him eagerly and asked where he had been. He replied that he had been in court, pleading their cause against the Savior, and that he had won the case, meaning that they would not be burned.[30] In some of the trials, God and the Devil dispute claims to the souls of mankind in a series of legal quibbles. In others, God is the judge, Satan the prosecuting attorney, and the Blessed Virgin the advocate for the defense. In France as in some other European Kingdoms, the queen actually held an important position in the judicial system, and she could be petitioned to intercede for defendants. Terrestrial queens may have inspired the judicial role imagined for the Queen of Heaven.[31] In a juristic fantasy, *The Trial of Satan*, ascribed to the great writer of Roman Law, Bartolus of Sassoferrato, who revived jurisprudence at Perugia, Satan objected that the Virgin Mary must not be admitted to the bar as an advocate: first, because no woman was eligible to be a barrister, and second, because of her kinship to the Judge. Since the Judge was her son, the hearing would be biased. Mary responded to the objection by warning her son to ignore that shyster, who made quibbling allegations to cause confusion, and she urged him to get on with the case.[32]

Legal imagery pervaded medieval ideas about the relation to Satan. In verse and fable, "the Devil is very careful to establish his title to the soul of man by a faultless legal document," in later centuries signed in blood.[33] The Faust legend is the most familiar story of a pact with the Devil, but that was preceded by the story of Theophilus the Penitant.[34] Faust was a heroic figure of grand proportions, but Theophilus was a little man, not a gifted scholar in search of universal knowledge, but merely a frustrated bureaucrat. His story could serve as a model for the subtitle of Hannah Arendt's book on Adolph Eichmann: "the banality of evil."

According to the story, which was one of the best-known romances in the Middle Ages, frequently represented not only in folk lore, but also in sculpture and on painted glass, Theophilus was a church administrator in Cilicia around 538, during the reign of Justinian and a few years before the Persian invasion. He was known for his piety, his competence as an administrator, and his liberality to the poor.[35] When the post of bishop fell vacant, he was urged by the people as well as the church officials to occupy the office, but he refused out of feelings of humility. Someone else was raised to the seat, and later, hearing false rumors against Theophilus, the new bishop removed the latter from his administrative post. Hurt and brooding, Theophilus made a pact with Satan through a necromancer to get his job back. The pact with the Devil was inscribed on parchment and signed in blood. Subsequently, the bishop restored Theophilus to his old position, and the people cheered. Then, conscience got the best of Theophilus and allowed him no rest. He resolved on a solemn fast, praying in church all night. During his long vigil, the Blessed Virgin appeared one night, listened to his pleas for mercy, and agreed to intercede for him. The next night she reappeared and assured him that Christ had forgiven his sins. He woke with a cry of joy and found on his breast the document that had deeded his soul to the Devil. Without the contract, the Devil held no power over him. The next Sunday, Theophilus confessed in public during the liturgy, and displayed the contract, recovered from the Evil One by the mercy of the Mother of God. The bishop gave him absolution, and presided over the public burning of the document. Theophilus received communion, left the church in a fever, and died three days later.[36]

Although the story is probably a religious romance, the *Acta Sanctorum* include Theophilus as a saint, honoring him on February 4. The legend was first written in Greek by Eutychian, who claimed to have lived in the house of Theophilus and to write from personal experience of the events. It was translated into Latin by Paul the Deacon in the 8th century, dramatized in the 10th century by Hrosvitha, the illustrious nun of Gandersheim in Saxony, and inspired a number of morality plays, perhaps ultimately suggesting the Faust theme. The iconography of Theophilus is extensive, and the legend often appears in stone, including two representations in the cathedral of Notre-Dame in Paris.

A detail of the central sculpture of the north transept tympanum of Notre Dame, made around 1250, shows the story in four scenes. The first scene shows Theophilus kneeling, pledging fealty by placing his folded hands between the palms of the Devil. The last scene shows the Virgin wielding a cross to threaten Satan, who crouches before her and surrenders the contract. The earliest image of the Theophilus legend appears in a sculptured relief on the tympanum of a portal in the domed church of Souillac, a Romanesque structure completed around 1130 in southern France.[37]

The sculptured relief at Souillac appears over an arched portal. Two lower figures flanking the arch are Old Testament representations: Joseph on the left, Isaiah on the right. To the right of Isaiah stands a sculptured column, an intricate *trumeau* of straining, tangled figures. The face of the *trumeau* is covered by interlocking beasts, men, reptiles, and monsters devouring one another. The central scene over the arch represents three episodes in the life of Theophilus. The flanking figures of St. Benedict on the left and St. Peter on the right place the scene in the context of ecclesiastical administration.[38]

A detail of the central field shows two pairs of figures in the lower register: two representations of the Devil and Theophilus. The images of the Devil show an emaciated body with visible ribs, the hideous head of a monster, and, indeed, the spurs of a cock on the calves of his legs. The feet are different in each scene, and the Devil on the right has the claw of a predatory bird for one foot and a cloven hoof for the other. In the left pair, the Devil and Theophilus are holding the document and drawing up their legal contract. In the right pair, the Devil is grasping the hands of Theophilus between his own, making him his liege man in a ceremonial gesture of feudal homage. In the upper register, the final scene, which transcends the others, the Queen of Heaven and an angel are descending to the sleeping-praying Theophilus, who lies adjacent to the church in which he spent his vigil of forty nights. The Holy Mother is returning the contract, assisted by an angel who has one hand on her shoulder and the other on Theophilus. In all three scenes, the most important images are dominated by legal symbols—the document of the pact and the feudal oath of fealty.

The legalistic imagery of the Middle Ages turned the forces of evil into a vast spiritual underworld, permitted within limits to act in nature on men. The divine purpose was to test the loyalty of men and to strengthen their moral fiber in the crucible of temptation. The essentials of the theory of nature implied in the cosmology and demonology were spelled out by St. Augustine. Centuries later, the treatises and manuals on witchcraft—Lea lists about forty of them in his materials on the history of witchcraft—may be understood as footnotes to the work of Augustine. The *Malleus Maleficarum,* or "Hammer of Witches," published around 1486 by the inquisitors, Sprenger and Kramer, provided the model for this literature. The *Malleus,* incidentally, was one of the first books to be printed in pocket editions. Judges and lawyers questioned the accused with their copies of the *Malleus* ready for reference under the table or up their sleeves. Lea writes that the *Malleus* acquired such great authority that it "fastened on European jurisprudence for nearly three centuries the duty of combating the devil and saving mankind from his clutches."[39]

During the peak of the witchcraft trials, animals shared some of the burden of persecution.[40] Pigs suffered the most, since it was thought they were especially vulnerable to demonic possession. The legion of devils that had entered the herd of Gadarene swine in the New Testament story, it was remembered, had said to Jesus, "Send us among the pigs and let us go into them" (Mark 5: 12). Pigs ran freely in the streets of medieval towns and often got into trouble. Besides, animals were often distinguished as "sweet beasts" or "stenchy beasts." The hart and the hind, panting after the flowing brooks as the soul thirsts for the living God, as the Psalmist said, led the list of sweet beasts. The pig, of course, led the stenchy beasts. Goats and polecats provided other stenchy habitats enjoyed by unclean spirits.

Pigs were often judged for injuring and sometimes killing children. In 1386, a sow of Falaise that had attacked and killed a child was mutilated and then executed in the village square, dressed up as a human being. The expense of the case included a pair of new gloves for the executioner, so that he might come out with clean hands. Even though pigs were rarely shown mercy, in one case youth was a reason for clemency, when in 1457 at Lavegny, a sow and her litter were charged with having murdered and partially devoured a child. The sow was condemned to death, but the piglets were released because of their tender age and because their mother had set them a bad example.[41]

An execution without a proper trial could stir a great deal of indignation. In 1576 in Schweinfurt in Franconia, a sow that had mutilated a child was delivered into custody. Without legal authority, the executioner "hanged it publicly to the disgrace and detriment of the city." The hangman was forced to flee and never dared to return. The case gave rise to the proverbial phrase, *"Schweinfurter Sauhenker,"* meaning "sow hanger from Schweinfurt," used to characterize a ruffian and vile sort of fellow. As Evans wrote, "It was not the mere killing of the sow, but the execution without a judicial decision, the insult and contempt of the magistracy and the judicatory by arrogating their functions, that excited the public wrath and official indignation."[42]

As Needham has shown, the frequency of animal trials followed a curve rising from three recorded instances in the 9th century, to a peak of about sixty in the 16th century, dropping to nine cases in the 19th century. They fall into three types: one, actions against domestic animals for attacking human beings (e.g., the execution of pigs for devouring infants); two, actions against swarms, resulting in anathemas or excommunicatory rituals—a kind of spiritual pesticide; and three, the condemnation of lusus naturae: e.g., the laying of eggs by putative roosters.[43]

The animal trials collected by Evans (1906) account for more than two hundred cases extending over a thousand years. The latest in his record, the case of a dog executed in Switzerland for homicide, took place in 1906, the very year the book went to press. Some celebrated cases were located in Switzerland and France, but the list names a large number of Occidental countries, including Belgium, Denmark, Germany, Italy, Portugal, Russia, Spain, Turkey, England, Scotland, Canada, and the United States.[44] A whole range of insects and animals were brought to the bar of justice, "including asses, beetles, bloodsuckers, bulls, caterpillars, cockchafers . . . cows, dogs, dolphins, eels, field mice, flies, goats, grasshoppers, horses, locusts, mice, moles, rats, serpents, sheep, slugs, snails, swine, termites, turtledoves, weevils, wolves, worms, and nondescript vermin." The most common defendants were pigs, for reasons I have discussed. The condemned animals were dispatched in various ways, depending on the local forms of punishment. The Russians, for example, continued to use banishment in one or two cases, and at the end of the 17th century, the record shows a billy goat exiled to Siberia.[45]

Karl von Amira, a historian of law writing at the end of the 19th century, insisted on a technical distinction between secular animal punishments for crimes such as homicide, and ecclesiastical animal trials. The trials, he showed, led back to the demonology of the Middle Ages,[46] and were associated with certain formal adjurations, particularly the maledictio and the anathema found in the ritual of excommunication, as well as the more familiar rite of exorcism. These procedures were directed not primarily at the animals on trial, but at the evil spirits believed to inhabit them. The ritual was intended to prevent further devastation of orchards, vineyards, and fields, and to halt the depletion of soil and water by the action of noxious vermin possessed by demons. The effectiveness of the imprecation or interdiction depended on the proper judicial ritual. In other words, these supernatural sanctions were not expected to work without due process of law. Evans showed, "Before fulminating an excommunication the whole machinery of justice was put into motion in order to establish the guilt of the accused, who were then warned, admonished, and threatened. . . ."[47]

In the tenth century, the pious Archbishop of Trèves was saying mass in the church of St. Peter when an irreverent swallow dipped and soared over his head. If he enjoyed a halo, it offered no protection against this winged creature, for it defecated on the venerable head, and the holy man transcended his piety to roar an excommunication. From that moment, swallows kept scrupulously out of the building, leaving in peace the worshippers within, and if one of them intruded into the entry, it promptly fell dead upon the pavement. A case still better known is recorded for the 11th century. St. Bernard, preaching in the monastery at Foigny, which he had founded, was tormented by the flies buzzing around his head. He shouted at them, "I excommunicate you!" The flies fell on the floor in heaps so high that shovels were needed to get rid of them.[48] The case of the Flies at Foigny became so well known that the only point left open for speculation was the question of how long it took for the flies to experience the impact of the excommunication. The flies had been executed without due process of law, but the chronicler explains that the situation was desperate and no other remedy at hand.

In the early part of the 16th century, Bartholomew Chasseneux, the leading authority on ritual procedures against animals, became one of the most distinguished jurists in France. Starting out as an advocate in Bourgogne, he was elected in 1531 to the rank of counselor in the *Parlement de Paris,* and in the following year appointed to the *Parlement de Provence,* where he held the post of Premier Président, a position equivalent to the rank of Chief Justice. Chasseneux was the author of a wide-ranging work he called *A Catalogue of the Glories of the World,* and he was also known as a commentator of the customary law of Burgundy. A collection of seventy-nine of his principal *consilia* appeared in 1531,[49] and the first *Consilium* in this collection became his most celebrated work. It was a lengthy, definitive treatise explaining and justifying the procedures of excommunication against animals and insects. He provided a long list of cases, beginning with the cursing of the serpent in the Garden of Eden, in which anathemas and excommunications had worked against creatures that crawl and creep and fly. This treatise, the *Consilium Primum,* established his eminence as a theorist, but he won his laurels as a barrister from his work in a celebrated trial before the ecclesiastical court of Autun. In that trial, and in similar cases that followed, he made a brilliant reputation defending rats. As Evans put it, "the ingenuity and acumen with which Chasseneux conducted the defence, the legal learning which he brought to bear on the case, and the eloquence of his plea enlisted the public interest and established his fame as a criminal lawyer and forensic orator."[50] Lest you think there was nothing extraordinary in a criminal lawyer making a brilliant career defending rats, you must understand that they were four-legged rats.

The rats were being charged with devouring the barley crop in the countryside of Burgundy. The people, complaining that the infestation was intolerable, petitioned the bishop to excommunicate the varmints. The episcopal court, knowing Chasseneux's reputation as an expert on spiritual pesticides, appointed him as defense attorney to the rats. He prepared the case with great skill. It was believed that no excommunication or other adjuration against animals could be effective unless the beasts had been provided with a proper and scrupulous legal defense.

Chasseneux's first maneuver was to challenge the summons. He argued that the rats had a bad name and suffered the disability of having public opinion against them. They were improperly summoned, because they were dispersed all over the countryside, dwelling in numerous villages, and a single summons was insufficient to notify them all. The second citation, then, was read from the pulpits of every parish inhabited by the rats. This proclamation took more time, and at the end of the period assigned, the rats still did not appear. Chasseneux argued that since there were so many rats living in so many places, great preparations were necessary for a mass migration, and this required more time. When the rats still did not appear, he got an additional postponement, and excused the default of his clients on the grounds that their journey was difficult and made hazardous by the presence of their natural enemies, the cats. These mortal foes of the rats, Chasseneux contended, watched all their movements and lay in wait for them at every turn. He showed that a proper summons implied the right of safe conduct, and that if the way were full of peril and without protection, the defendants were justified in not obeying the writ. Finally, he demanded that the plaintiffs—the farmers—be required under bond to prevent their cats from frightening the rats. The plaintiffs demurred, but the case moved from one delay to another. The record does not tell us who won, but it is safe to infer that the rats eventually lost by default, and that ultimately an excommunication was fulminated against them.[51]

Throughout the Middle Ages, treatises were written to protest the absurdity of animal trials, most of them criticizing the folly of maledictions, anathemas, and excommunications against pests. Occasionally, a prelate would forbid fulminations against animals without special permission or specific license.[52] Some Spanish theologians were prone to dismiss the trials as vain and superstitious,[53] arguing that insects, being devoid of reason, cannot comprehend the meaning of prayers and curses launched at them, and since their depredation is caused by their natural appetites, and since they have no free will, they were not guilty of sin. Joseph Needham suggests that the medieval attitude wavered: "Sometimes the field-mice or locusts were considered to be breaking God's laws, and therefore subject to prosecution and conviction by man, while at other times the view prevailed that they had been sent to admonish men to repentence and amendment."[54]

I believe that the medieval attitude was not a single wavering viewpoint, but a triad of contrary positions. One position considered the animals hungry creatures of God, with neither reason nor responsibility, simply following the inclinations given to them by nature. The second position considered them instruments of God, sent to punish a community for some sin committed by the inhabitants. The third position viewed them as the temporary vehicles of demons or as instruments of the Devil. The first two positions implied decent treatment: they were persuaded to stop their devastation and given another place to go. The third required some kind of exorcism, or some kind of powerful intervention. The argument for the prosecution proceeded from the third position. The defense argued from the first or the second, sometimes both.

It was an empirical question in each case to determine if the animals were acting simply as creatures, or as special instruments of God, or as the instruments of evil spirits. Anathemas hurled at the animals were directed inferentially at the Devil or at the demons contained within them. Thomas Aquinas argued that it was either blasphemous or vain to curse beasts if they were agents of God or simply creatures behaving according to instinct. They were properly cursed only if they were agents of Satan and inspired by the powers of hell.[55]

Every animal trial tested natural phenomena to ascertain if they represented divine agency, diabolic agency, or nature working alone. Just as witchcraft cases placed phenomena on trial, so also animal trials sought confirmation of one of the three hypotheses. Moreover, the trials of delinquent animals as well as witches were forums in which lawyers and judges argued the precise location of the boundaries between natural and supernatural events.

In his book on the decline of witchcraft trials in France, Robert Mandrou (1968) shows the importance of those trials in establishing a line of demarcation between the natural and the supernatural, and also shows how the trials provided the occasion for lawyers, judges, priests, physicians, and scientists to collaborate in that "collective adventure" that a "spiritual revolution" represents.[56] Out of that collaboration in the 17th century there emerged a new jurisprudence, a new theory of abnormal psychological states, and a new view of natural processes. The magistrates of the sovereign courts, Mandrou demonstrates, in their new integration of medical knowledge and theology, occupied the first rank in the progress of rationalism in 17th century France.

In the past three centuries, the most striking change, Lecky tells us, may be found in the common response to the idea of the miraculous. Now, when the spirit of rationalism predisposes men to attribute all kinds of phenomena to natural rather than to miraculous causes, the account of a miracle would draw "an absolute and even derisive incredulity which dispenses with all examination of the evidence." To ascribe unexplainable phenomena to supernatural agency "is beyond the range of reasonable discussion." In contrast, a few centuries before, miraculous accounts were not only credible but ordinary.[57] The vocabulary of disenchantment provided alternative expressions for experiences that had previously been identified by names for supernatural or preternatural agency.

The great astronomer, Johannes Kepler, helped to invent the scientific idiom of disenchantment by repudiating the old animistic ideas of planetary motion. Before Kepler, celestial motion was believed to be the product of souls or minds, usually represented as divine agencies.[58] Kepler used the term "force or energy"—*vis seu energia*—to explain the movement of the planets.[59] He did not invent the Latin word *vis*, but before him, Pliny in his *Natural History*, which appeared about 77 A.D. and remained one of the most important scientific works of the ancient world, had used the term *vis* in a very general and ambiguous way, to mean all kinds of forces, including psychic and occult effects as well as physical force. Kepler restricted the concept to mechanical force. He explicitly distinguished it from any kind of psychic, spiritual, or mental force.

In his *Epitome of Copernican Astronomy*, which completed publication in 1621, Kepler concluded that the motion of the planets was not the work of mind, as the ancients believed, but the work of the natural power of bodies.[60] The common practice of reducing celestial movement to the hidden forces of some soul, he wrote, was the sanctuary of all ignorance and the death of all philosophy. He preferred to think of the cause of planetary motion as impetus only—that is, as movement produced by "a uniform exertion of forces" (for "forces" he used the Latin word *virium*, the genitive plural of *vis*), without the work of mind.[61] In the same year,[62] he proposed that the word *vis*, which means "force," should replace the word *anima*, which means "soul." That substitution, Dijksterhuis observes, implies nothing less than "a radical revision of thought."[63] The action of "souls" in nature was understood by principles of magic. The laws of mechanics are expressed in the language of mathematics.

Kepler's substitution removed the magic from motion. In Collingwood's words, Kepler's "momentous step" of replacing *anima* by *vis* implied that "the conception of vital energy producing qualitative changes should be replaced by that of a mechanical energy, itself quantitative, and producing quantitative changes." Before that replacement, "man's mastery over nature was conceived not as the mastery of mind over mechanism but as the mastery of one soul over another soul, which implied magic. . . ."[64]

Albert Einstein, in his Preface to Kepler's *Life and Letters*, suggests that the two opposing principles of animism and mechanism struggled within Kepler, and that he never succeeded in entirely extricating himself from animistic thinking.[65] Max Caspar, Kepler's biographer, agrees that Kepler, who "founded the mechanistic explanation of the heavenly motions, remained suspended between an animistic and a mechanistic view of nature."[66] But Kepler remained enmeshed by animism in another way as well.

How does the Rooster of Basel, the victim of medieval animism, lead to Kepler, Needham asks. The answer is ironic, for Kepler suffered a narrow escape from similar victimization. In 1621, the *Epitome of Copernican Astronomy* completed publication, substituting the concept of *vis* for the concept of *anima*. But Kepler himself wrote about 1621: "I spent the whole year on my mother's trial."[67] His mother was being tried for witchcraft, and he had assumed the burden of preparing her legal defense. In a document of 128 pages, he did not deny a belief in witches—just as his British contemporary, Francis Bacon, did not deny it. Edward Rosen observes that "like many another great man in his time Kepler never expressed any disbelief in the existence of witches."[68] Caspar agrees that "the belief in demoniac influences and effects" remained part of Kepler's thinking.[69] Nevertheless, in his brief for the defense and in his bill of exceptions, he carefully accounted for every act for which his mother was being charged by referring it to a natural process. He drew the line and saved her life.

Caspar writes that after Kepler, a later era "raised the completely mechanistic explanation of the models of nature to a principle and, with a remarkable shyness of everything which is called soul, required, in the name of science, the weeding out of every psychic power."[70] This passage from animism to mechanism evolved through specific and remarkable historic occasions—juridical occasions as well as scientific. In Kepler's own words, which I take the liberty to translate from Latin: "To me, the occasions by which men arrive at the knowledge of celestial things seem no less astonishing than the very nature of celestial things."[71] The courts, I have argued, in the trials that tested demonic influences, provided some astonishing occasions for the progressive disenchantment of nature.

When nature is full of souls, their actions and the consequences of their behavior may be understood through moral categories. Spirits acting in nature were held personally responsible for certain natural phenomena. Kepler's substitution of *vis* for *anima*, extended from the celestial to the terrestrial sphere, does much more than submit nature to the languages of mathematics. It is also a declaration of the innocence of nature, or at least a proclamation that moral conceptual categories are irrelevant to the understanding of natural phenomena.

In the 17th century, animals still went on trial, but Racine wrote *The Litigants*, his only comedy, about a trial in which a dog is charged with stealing a capon, and when it was shown in 1668 it made Louis XIV laugh. In 1672, Colbert forbade the sovereign courts of France to hear cases of witchcraft.[72]

In the physical sciences, Newton drew a boundary line and stood on it like Janus, with faces to both centuries. Keynes called him "the last of the magicians."[73] As Keynes observed, Newton dropped the 17th century behind him and became the 18th century figure, which is the unmagical, traditional Newton—the sage of the Age of Reason.

At the end of his eight-volume *History of Magic and Experimental Science*, Lynn Thorndike breathed a sigh of relief and concluded, "animism had been replaced by mechanism." As he explained, "a dividing line had been drawn between science and superstition which was sharper and more satisfactory than any that had been previously attempted. . . . The boundaries of natural and experimental science seemed to be more distinctly defined than they ever had been before. They had been so drawn as to lie outside theology as well as of magic, and to exclude miracles, demons and diabolical or spiritual action as well as other forms of the occult."[74]

The courtroom exploration of demonological issues had helped settle those boundaries. It had inspired a collective effort of reinterpretation and disenchantment: a radical revision of thought. It helped change the contours of animistic thinking so that it did not remain what Gaston Bachelard called an "epistemological obstacle" to the scientific world view.[75] Instead, the legalistic demonology of Christian animism shaped a forensic matrix for the expression of scientific thought and for its extension beyond the boundaries of science. Within that matrix, lawyers and judges, who were in touch with the changing scientific currents of the 16th and 17th centuries, carried on debates about the boundaries of nature. Within that matrix we may trace the changing map of the universe.

NOTES

1. E. P. Evans, *The Criminal Prosecution and Capital Punishment of Animals* (New York: Dutton, 1906), p. 162. Joseph Needham, *Science and Civilisation in China*, Vol. II (Cambridge: Cambridge University Press, 1969), p. 574.

2. Evans, p. 162.

3. P. A. Robin, *Animal Lore in English Literature* (London: Murray, 1932), pp. 84–95.

4. L. J. Cole, "The Lay of the Rooster," *Journal of Heredity* 18 (1927):97–105.

5. Cole, p. 99.

6. Cole, p. 99.

7. Cole, p. 100.

8. Cole, p. 105.

9. Needham, *Science and Civilisation*, II, p. 575.

10. Joseph Needham, *Clerks and Craftsmen in China and the West* (Cambridge: Cambridge University Press, 1970), p. 310.

11. Needham, *Science and Civilisation*, II, p. 518.

12. Needham, *Science and Civilisation*, II, p. 582.

13. Needham, *Science and Civilisation*, II, p. 291.

14. Needham, *Science and Civilisation*, II, p. 286.

15. Needham, *Science and Civilisation*, II, p. 582; *The Grand Titration* (London: Allen & Unwin, 1969), p. 330.

16. Needham, *The Grand Titration*, p. 330.

17. Werner Heisenberg, *The Physicist's Conception of Nature*, tr. by A. J. Pomerans (New York: Harcourt, Brace, 1958), p. 15, ital. removed.

18. Heisenberg, *The Physicist's Conception of Nature*, p. 29, ital. in the original.

19. William James, *The Varieties of Religious Experience* (New York: Modern Library, 1902).

20. S. Nakayama and N. Sivin, *Chinese Science* (Cambridge: M.I.T. Press, 1973), pp. 206–207.

21. Max Weber, *The Religion of China*, tr. by H. H. Gerth (New York: Free Press, 1951), pp. 153, 206, 228.

22. Henry Charles Lea, *A History of the Inquisition of Spain*, Vol IV (New York: Macmillan, 1907), p. 207.

23. Edward Langton, *Essentials of Demonology* (London: Epworth, 1949), p. 29.

24. Lynn White, Jr., "Natural Science and Naturalistic Art in the Middle Ages," *American Historical Review* 52 (1947):421–435.

25. White, "Natural Science," p. 435.

26. G. G. Coulton, *Five Centuries of Religion*, Vol. I (Cambridge: Cambridge University Press, 1923), p. 66.

27. Henry Osborn Taylor, *The Mediaeval Mind*, Vol. I, 4th ed. (Cambridge: Harvard University Press, 1949), p. 504.

28. Coulton, *Five Centuries*, p. 62.

29. Coulton, *Five Centuries*, pp. 466–467.

30. Coulton, *Five Centuries*, pp. 65–66.

31. Meyer Shapiro, "The Sculpture of Souillac," in *Medieval Studies in Memory of A. Kingsley Porter*, ed. by W. R. W. Koehler, Vol. II (Cambridge: Harvard University Press, 1939), p. 379.

32. Coulton, *Five Centuries*, p. 64.

33. Paul Carus, *The History of the Devil and the Idea of Evil* (New York: Land's End Press, 1969, 1st pub. 1900), p. 414.

34. J. B. Russell, *Witchcraft in the Middle Ages* (Ithaca: Cornell University Press, 1972), p. 19.

35. A. C. Fryer, "Theophilus, The Penitent, as Represented in Art," *Archaeological Journal* 92 (1935):287–333. S. Baring-Gould, *The Lives of the Saints*, 3rd ed., Vol. II (Edinburgh: Grant, 1914), pp. 88–91.

36. S. Baring-Gould, *Curious Myths of The Middle Ages*, Second Series (London: Rivingtons, 1868), pp. 363–370.

37. Schapiro, "The Sculpture," p. 380. Fryer, "Theophilus,' p. 289. Paul Deschamps, *French Sculpture of the Romanesque Period: Eleventh and Twelfth Centuries* (New York: Hacker Art Books, 1972), p. 27.

38. Schapiro, "The Sculpture," p. 378.

39. Henry Charles Lea, *Materials Toward a History of Witchcraft*, Vol. I (Philadelphia: University of Pennsylvania Press, 1939), p. 305.

40. Evans. *The Criminal Prosecution*, p. 165.

41. E. A. Westermarck, *The Origin and Development of the Moral Ideas*, Vol. I (London: Macmillan, 1912), p. 257.

42. Evans, *The Criminal Prosecution*, p. 147.

43. Needham, *Science and Civilisation*, II, p. 574. *The Grand Titration*, p. 328.

44. W. W. Hyde, "The Prosecution and Punishment of Animals and Lifeless Things in the Middle Ages and Modern Times," *University of Pennsylvania Law Review* 64 (1916):709.

45. Hyde, "The Prosecution," p. 712.

46. Karl von Amira, *Thierstrafen und Thierprocesse* (Innsbruck: Verlag der Wagner' schen Universitäts-Buchhandlung, 1891), p. 548.

47. Evans, *The Criminal Prosecution*, p. 4.

48. Henry Charles Lea, *Studies in Church History* (Philadelphia: Henry C. Lea's Son & Co., 1883), pp. 428–429.

49. J-H. Pignot, *Un jurisconsulte au seizième siècle: Barthélemy de Chasseneuz* (Paris: Larose, 1880), p. 211.

50. Evans, *The Criminal Prosecution*, p. 21.

51. Evans, pp. 18–19. Hyde, "The Prosecution," pp. 706–707. Lea, *Studies in Church History*, p. 430. S. Baring-Gould, *Curiosities of Olden Times*, Rev. ed. (Edinburgh: Grant, 1896), p. 65.

52. Baring-Gould, *Curiosities*, p. 67.

53. Lea, *Studies in Church History*, p. 432.

54. Needham, *The Grand Titration*, p. 330.

55. Evans, *The Criminal Prosecution*, pp. 54–55.

56. Robert Mandrou, *Magistrats et sorciers en France au XVIIe siècle* (Paris: Librairie Plon, 1968), p. 564.

57. W. E. H. Lecky, *History of the Rise and Influence of the Spirit of Rationalism in Europe*, Vol. I (New York: Appleton, 1868), p. 17, 27.

58. Max Jammer, *Concepts of Force* (Cambridge: Harvard University Press, 1957), p. 51.

59. Jammer, p. 87.

60. Johannes Kepler, *Epitome Astronomiae Copernicae, Opera Omnia*, ed. by C. Frisch, Vol. VI (Frankfurt and Erlangen: Heyder & Zimmer, 1866), p. 372.

61. Kepler, p. 393.

62. Jammer, *Concepts of Force*, p. 90, refers to a note that appeared in the second edition of *Mysterium cosmographicum*.

63. E. J. Dijksterhuis, *The Mechanization of the World Picture* tr. by C. Dikshoorn (London: Oxford University Press, 1961), p. 310.

64. R. G. Collingwood, *The Idea of Nature* (London: Oxford University Press, 1945), p. 102, 96.

65. Carola Baumgardt, *Johannes Kepler: Life and Letters* (New York: Philosophical Library, 1951).

66. Max Caspar, *Kepler*, tr. by C. D. Hellman (London and New York: Abelard-Schuman, 1959), p. 383.

67. Johannes Kepler, *Somnium*, tr. by Edward Rosen (Madison: University of Wisconsin Press, 1967, 1st publ 1634), p. xix.

68. Edward Rosen, "Kepler and Witchcraft Trials," *The Historian* 28 (1966):449.

69. Caspar, *Kepler*, p. 240.

70. Caspar, p. 384.

71. Alexander Koyré, *The Astronomical Revolution*, tr. by R. E. W. Maddison (London: Methuen, 1973), p. 119.

72. Jules Michelet, *Satanism and Witchcraft*, tr. by A. R. Allinson (Secanius, NJ: Lyle Stuart, 1939), p. xx.

73. J. M. Keynes, *New Tercentenary Celebration* (London: Royal Society, 1947).

74. Lynn Thorndike, *A History of Magic and Experimental Science*, Vol. VIII (New York: Columbia University Press, 1923–1958), p. 604.

75. Gaston Bachelard, *La formation de l'esprit scientifique*, 6th ed. (Paris: J. Vrin, 1969).

6. The Mathematical Model in Plato and Some Surrogates in a Jain Theory of Knowledge*

Edith Wyschogrod

One of the generative questions in Benjamin Nelson's late work was: What accounts for the breakthrough insights which permit the reduction of all quality to quantity, the proclaiming of a mathematical reality behind the experiential immediacies of experience, and the affirmation of a homogeneous time and space the same throughout the universe, insights which characterize Western science. It is a question that simultaneously exercized Nelson and Joseph Needham, both consider it from an inter-civilizational perspective. To put the matter in Needham's terms: "What was it that happened in Renaissance Europe when mathematics and science joined in a combination qualititatively new and destined to transform the world?"[1]

Nelson first answers these questions by examining Western orientations and institutions of the twelfth and thirteenth centuries. He shows that in a "sacro-magical if sacramentalized" reading of creator and cosmos "there appears a stress upon the need and ability of men to know and explain natural phenomena by the principles of natural philosophy, to offer rational justification of their acts and opinions."[2] In the same context Nelson speaks of a two-fold commitment to the "concrete individual person," and to an "objective Universal." Armed with Nelson's questions (the subject of fruitful conversations long before the appearance of the article cited) I pondered the issues of whether these factors, already nascent in the epistemic structure of Plato's dialogues concerned with the Ideas, could not be displayed against an Indian system remarkably similar in hierarchical structure and philosophic intent. For, I thought,

---

*This paper was first presented at the meeting of the International Society for the Comparative Study of Civilizations (U. S.) at Bradford College, Haverhill, Massachusetts in April 1977.

only in the light of these similarities would the key difference—the existence of an "objective Universal" in one and not the other—emerge. The same aim governs both the Platonic and Jain epistemologies, the overcoming of sense experience in order to attain a more adequate access route to truth. But, in the former, structures of universalization—the ideas of number and geometric form—lead to this overcoming while in the latter certain *ad hoc* extensions of sense itself are made to play this part. My paper in no way attempts to ground larger claims such as the existence of an ongoing tradition unbroken from Plato to the twelfth century. Nelson would be the first to puncture so ominously unhistorical a claim. I attempt rather to bring out the difference between a system which engages the constructs of a contemporary mathematics and eventuates in an *objective* Universal and one which fails to do so.

Both Plato and a Jain text, *The Tattvarthadhigama Sutra* of Śri Umasvati with the commentary of Śri Pujyapada,[3] argue that the knowledge of sensibles is merely preliminary to higher forms of knowing and that these in turn culminate in a highest or ultimate form of knowledge. Furthermore both the Jain and Platonic systems concur in claiming necessity, apodicticity and comprehensiveness or totalizing power for such knowledge. In the light of these common considerations I argue here that a difference in what are considered possible objects of knowledge by each system accounts for the positing of differently conceived faculties of knowledge. I argue further that the faculties alleged to attain higher knowledge in Jain epistemology are compatible with the Jain understanding of the objects of knowledge. Thus an internally consistent account of knowing is provided in a scheme which assumes a) the actuality of the material world but b) presupposes that knowledge of the world in some sense falls short of ultimate truth and c) lacks mathematical paradigms for providing a means of transition between the world of ordinary experience and that of final knowledge.

In order to support these claims it is important to clarify in advance how the possible objects of knowledge are understood in each system and how the transition from lower to higher knowledge is effected. In the Platonic account the move from lower to higher epistemological levels is achieved by conferring a unique status upon a class of objects, number and figure, which facilitates a transition between apprehension of the empirical world and the world of Ideas. When applied to practical ends these objects are still encumbered by visible images but when divested of their concrete applications they are themselves Ideas. The assumptions of arithmetic and geometry do not themselves constitute the ultimate ground of certainty, for mathematical hypotheses which may appear certain to the mathematical sciences must be subjected to philosophical analysis. Ultimate knowledge involves the systematic relationship and harmony of the world of Forms in their hierarchical nature and as they control the world of experience. Mathematical knowledge is seen both as the model for and the prolegomenon to this ultimate vision.

The Tattvarthadhigama Sutra shares at least this basic assumption with the Platonic view: namely that there is a duplicity of Being which generates the appearance of things as multiple and temporal. However multiplicity and temporality themselves are not interpreted as giving rise to the notion of objects as numerable, to the operation of counting as such, leading in turn to a conception of number which can be freed from its empirical context.[4] In consequence the transcendence of the spatio-temporal order must be achieved by the attempt to acquire transcendent knowledge without recourse to elements and relations other than those immediately given, those which the spatio-temporal continuum itself directly presents. The conditions for transcending the spatio-temporal world are seen as lodged within the perimeter of the world. Jain ontology presumes the materiality of the world (including not only matter but time, space and motion among its elements).[5] No tertiary class of entities, that is entities which are neither material (in the broad sense suggested) nor spiritual, is predicated. Thus no object comparable to number and figure incorporating both the permanence and stability of the ideal realm and the multiplicity of the sensible realm is introduced. Only the world itself can be predicated as the object of knowing through which access to higher forms of knowledge can be acquired.

One further point remains to be clarified before pressing the claim that, despite their common supposition that knowledge of sensibles is preliminary to higher knowledge, the ontological status and character ascribed to the objects of knowledge in each system will determine the ground and structure of the faculties needed for the apprehension of these objects. This point relates to the Jain understanding of the ontology of sensibles. In the context of ordinary experience physical objects are so arranged that they appear to be governed by inviolable rules such as the rule that it is impossible for an observer to both be and not be in the same place at a given instant. The Jain system supposes that the laws governing temporal sequentiality and spatial contiguity are viable within the context of ordinary experience, but *relevant only to it*. No immutable laws of nature such as are assumed by Platonic or Aristotelean metaphysics which would militate against the disruption of the perceived order of the world are presupposed. The spatio-temporal order of nature is seen as applicable within the parameters set by sense experience but is nowhere interpreted as having eternal and necessary status.[6]

Since, as we have already seen, no entities comparable to mathematical objects are posited the world of sensibles remains the only object of knowledge. Thus a faculty which could provide the transition from lower to higher knowledge must have the world (of objects and persons, etc.) as its only cognitive sphere. Furthermore that faculty need not be governed by the laws that sense perception leads one to believe are inherent in the nature of things. Having laid down these premises, it becomes possible to posit "supernormal" powers (clairvoyance and telepathy) as faculties which can mediate the transition from sense perception to the final phase of knowledge, omniscience.[7] These powers function as epistemological alternatives to the mathematical model in Plato's account of knowing in the sense of providing a link between graded levels of knowledge. But rather than multiplying entities (as the ontological status conferred upon Mathematical Ideas compels us to do) the Jain model assumes the permeability of the physical and mental (a quasi-physical concept)[8] worlds to Spirit so that the occult powers predicated enable the adept to penetrate the physical order.

The epistemological course chosen by Plato is to posit objects which are neither entities found in the world nor mental "objects" corresponding to them. Thus existents need not be "penetrated" or rearranged. Plato's account of knowledge seeks to resolve the perplexity arising from "the sea of change" *by diverting attention from the world of aisthesis,* that is from "the world of sensations and judgments in accordance with them."[9] Arithmetic as the science of number has this salutary effect for its objects lack specific referents: "Arithmetic has a very great and elevating effect compelling the soul to reason about abstract number, and rebelling against the introduction of visible or tangible objects into the argument."[10] Geometry, while making use of visible forms and reasoning about them is not thinking about these "but of the ideals which they resemble, not of" the figure geometers draw but of the absolute square and the absolute diameter.[11] The positing of mathematical objects makes it possible for the mind to become the percipient rather than the eye.

For the *Tattvarthadhigama Sutra* and its commentator the soul's percipience depends not upon the ontological status of the object beheld but upon the elimination of karmic accumulation from the soul. Karma is specific to the various modes of cognition. Thus to attain supernormal powers the karma appropriate to preceding modes of cognition in addition to the karma obscuring the power that the knower wishes to achieve must be eliminated in order to "cut through" the world of perception.[12] Compare Socrates' view of the soul's function:

But in my opinion, that knowledge only which is of being and of the unseen can make the world look upwards, and whether a man gapes at the heavens or blinks on the ground, seeking to learn some particular of sense, I would deny that he can learn, for nothing of that sort is a matter of science; his soul is looking downwards and not upwards whether his way to knowledge is by water or by land, whether he floats or only lies on his back.[13]

with that of Śrī Pujyapada:

The disciple asks the saint with reverence, "O master, what is good for the soul?" The Saint says, "Liberation." He again asks the saint "What is the nature of this liberation, and what is the way to attain it?" The saint answers, "Liberation is the attainment of an altogether different state of the soul, on the removal of all the impurities of karmic matter, and the body, characterized by all the inherent qualities of the soul such as knowledge and bliss free from pain and suffering."[14]

It is instructive from the standpoint of our argument (that objects of knowledge determine the character of the faculty which apprehends them) to notice the end or goal towards which knowledge in each case tends. For Plato the object of genuine knowledge is being and the unseen for which Mathematical Ideas provide the model. For Jain epistemology the end of knowledge is freedom from attachment to the body and liberation from the variety of standpoints according to which a thing may be viewed. A fundamental doctrine of the Jain system holds that since contradictory attributes may be predicated of a thing, no affirmation can be regarded as absolutely true or false, the truth or falsity of an affirmation depending upon the standpoint from which the affirmation is made. The liberated soul transcends the relativity of viewpoint provided by modes of knowledge less encompassing than total omniscience.[15] The motive that engenders the quest for knowledge is the desire for release, for the avoidance of pain, for infinite perception viz., for the knowledge of substance without reference to its shifting conditions or modes.

The notion of standpoints which govern the apprehension of truth at any given level of knowledge is foreign to Plato's conception of truth since it is precisely the independence of mathematical truths from the standpoint of the thinker and from the conditions of contingency inhering in the sensible world which confers certainty upon the objects of mathematics. While mathematics may be said to "liberate" from the world of sensible objects, the knowledge to which it provides a link is not that of undifferentiated oneness but rather to the hierarchically organized world of Forms governing the realm of experience.[16] The role of the Ideas is crucial in this connection for it is through the Ideas that the many particulars are integrated into a totalizing scheme: the many sensibles may be united through participation in a single Idea. While this doctrine is governed by the notion of "one over many" as Aristotle alleges, it need not be interpreted as presupposing that Plato understands the Ideas in a univocal sense. In fact a number of interpretations is proferred each of which can still be subsumed under the conception "one over many." Plato means to include as Ideas: ethical and aesthetic notions such as those of the Good, of Justice, of Beauty; Ideas of metaphysical notions such as the One and the Many, Being and Non-Being etc.; Mathematical Ideas such as those of the circle, the diameter etc. of the geometer and numbers such as two, three etc. of the arithmetician; Ideas of natural kinds such as man, stone, etc.; Ideas for kinds of manufactured objects, tables, chairs, beds etc.[17] In each of these instances Plato is guided by the notion that many particulars participate in a single Idea.

In Jain epistemology there are no such organizing archetypes enabling the lower to be taken up into the higher through participation (as the lower deriving its being from the higher). While Jain epistemology recognizes a number of cognitive modes—sense perception, scriptural knowledge, clairvoyance and telepathy[18]—no object of these modes serves simultaneously as an object of knowledge and an organizing principle for objects of an ontologically lower level. The indicator for epistemological difference is karma, since each cognitive mode is obscured by its own karmic variant.

Higher forms of cognition presuppose the destruction of karma so that the knowledge conferred by the higher faculties manifests itself upon the ground of the soul. Such knowledge is termed "direct" (without the intermediation of the sense organs) and eliminates the temporal and spatial sequentiality characteristic of indirect cognitive modes. Direct knowledge is seen to be independent of what we might term "incoming data." The data given to the higher faculties are not different in kind from those of sense experience and its derivatives: rather they are perceived without relation to events contiguous to the observer and organized without reference to the modes of organizing data characteristic of ordinary experience. It is thus not the character of the data which changes but rather their principles of organization.

It would seem that *the adept* apprehends data in their plenary presence but *we* take it that two independent series of data are juxtaposed so that two discrete series are experienced as a single event. Thus event A (let us say the death of a man in Bengal) belongs to a series of events (viewed spatially) that are accessible only to those in his immediate vicinity in Bengal. A quite different series of events is accessible to observer A' in Gujarat. Two series of events normally unconnected by relations of proximity are now linked through the interest of observer A' in the death of the man in Bengal. Clairvoyance enables the adept to implement his "interest" by bringing into contiguity in the mind of a single observer two disparate series. The power of the observer is able to transcend the normal relations of temporal and spatial sequentiality through the development of a power which no longer requires the presence of physical objects in order for perception of these objects to take place.

An analogous case is made for telepathy: one grasps what another is thinking without reference to spoken utterance. While the theoretical suppositions underlying the relations of language to thought are not stated in the *Tattvarthadhigama Sutra* nor in the commentary, it would appear (however) that thinking is an infra-auditory linguistic process, a form of speaking which can be understood by one who possesses the appropriate faculty.

It is instructive to notice how the Sutra regards specific types of clairvoyance and telepathy. Two modes of clairvoyance are posited, one based on birth the other produced by the tranquillization and annihilation of karmic matter depending upon merit.[19] There are also two varieties of telepathy: one "straight," the other "curved" or winding. "Straight" telepathy enables the adept to acquire knowledge of "speech, body and mind" when these are the objects in the mind of another. "Curved" telepathy need not have recourse to objects; it attains access to past and future. The temporal extensiveness of the two differs in that the former is alleged to cover only several births; its spatial range is thought to cover in distance from two to eight miles but not beyond it. The latter is said to cover from seven to eight births in the past and future of oneself and others and is said to range spatially from eight miles "up to the entire abode of human beings."[20]

The doctrine underlying these examples, namely that preceding existences can be recalled, ought not to be confused with the Platonic doctrine of recollection. In the *Meno* we notice that recollection is of principles, their application being a matter of deductive inference. Thus knowledge of the nature of squares and triangles enables one to deduce the relationship between the area of a square and the length of its sides and to then recognize that if one wishes to construct a square whose area will be twice the length of its sides one cannot do so by doubling the length of the sides.[21] For Plato knowledge derived from recollection does not yield information about sense experiences but knowledge of general principles.

Moreover, the primary purpose in introducing the recollection theory, as the *Phaedo* clearly establishes, is to demonstrate the pre-existence of the soul. In the *Phaedo* Plato presumes archetypal forms and copies which resemble them. An ideal standard must be known before a judgement can be made about sense particulars, that all sensible things aim at this standard but fall short of it,[22] and furthermore that we "acquire this knowledge before we were born, and were born having the use of it." The position is summarized thus:

> Then may we not say ... that ... there is an absolute beauty, and goodness, and an absolute essence of all things; and if this which is now discovered to have existed in our former state, we refer all our sensation, and with this compare them finding these ideas to be pre-existent and our inborn possessions—then our soul must have had a prior existence, but if not, there would be no force in the argument.[23]

It is only in the *Republic* that mathematical knowledge provides the same function as clairvoyance and telepathy in the Jain system, since it is here that mathematical knowledge is seen as the stepping stone between the world of appearances and that of intelligible forms. Here a new view of knowledge is put forward which assumes the centrality of dialectic, a method of philosophical analysis conducted without reliance upon the data of sense perception and credited with being able to arrive at unquestioned first principles. In the simile of the line, Plato divides the intelligible world into two regions: that of mathematics and that of dialectic, each characterized by methodological differences in the attainment of its conclusions. The former may still use visible representations of its constructs while the latter is occupied with purely intelligible forms.[24] Furthermore both begin from hypotheses, the mathematician treating them as if they were first principles and arriving at conclusions without questioning initial assumptions, the dialectician treating hypotheses as hypotheses and nothing more. Dialectic recognizes the tentative character of hypotheses and uses them only to arrive at first principles. It is then possible to retrace the steps involved in reverse order and thus, descending, to arrive at conclusions which are solidly founded.[25] Accordingly the verification of the principles of arithmetic and geometry is not a matter of probable induction starting from particular facts of sense experience but is obtained by logical deduction from self-evident first principles.

The Jain logician also recognizes deduction as a legitimate mode of inference. Thus (to cite a common example) observing smoke on the hill, and knowing the invariable concomitance of smoke and fire, we are led to conclude that there is fire in the hill. But, the Jain logician argues that the premises themselves are based on sense experience and therefore deductive inference counts as sense knowledge. The same karma which obstructs sense experience is also alleged to obstruct correct inference.

Such knowledge is, in fact, classified as "indirect" in contradistinction to clairvoyance and telepathy. Jain epistemology stresses that "sensory cognition, remembrance, recognition, induction and deduction are synonyms,"[26] since the karma obstructing each is of the same type. In this sense the Jain view is close to that of simple empiricism in maintaining that (short of omniscience) knowledge is based upon the percepts and their relations.

Despite its inner coherence, the difficulties of a scheme which depends upon the violation of basic physical principles is obvious. However the Jain system manages to maintain a certain economy by avoiding the multiplication of entities qualitatively different from those found in the world of appearances.[27] In the Platonic scheme not only are ideal entities posited such as the Mathematical Ideas but, to make sense of these, other additional entities are required. Aristotle argues that Plato considered it necessary to furnish ideal perfect instances of the Mathematical Ideas and so posited the existence of intermediate ideal objects, Mathematical Numbers, involving the existence of identical units which are multiple like sense particulars but share the mode of being of eidetic entities.[28] Mathematical Numbers thus removed some difficulties in the understanding of mathematical operations engendered by the view that Mathematical Ideas are themselves unique and nonassociable through arithmetic processes such as addition etc. Aristotle summarizes the case thus: "Some (Plato) say both kinds of numbers exist that which has a before and after being identical with Ideas and Mathematical Numbers being different from the Ideas and sensible things."[29] Aristotle characterizes the Mathematical Numbers as being made up of ideal units or ones each of which is identical with every other. "Mathematical Number is counted thus—after 1, 2 (which consists of another 1 besides the former 1) and 3 (which consists of another 1 besides those two), and the other numbers similarly." Comparable geometrical entities are also presumed to have been posited by Plato.[30]

This view of arithmetic structure permits solution of what has been called the "ontological methexis" problem, that is the question of how each object remaining solidary (monadic) can combine with other objects into groups or assemblages. The solution is suggested by the nature of Ideal and Mathematical Numbers. Existing objects can participate in a genus since the genus exhibits the mode of being of arithmos, that is it exhibits the mode of being of each ideal number, yet its members, like the homogeneous monads in the realm of Mathematical Number (which are themselves outside change and time) can nevertheless be arranged into definite numbers.[31] It is clear that for Plato the sense world is transcended by organizing the multiplicity of sensibles into more comprehensive assemblages and by using the objects of arithmetic and geometry to provide a model for the world of Forms. The Jain scheme depends on no such model for its assumption is that while knowledge of sensibles can become increasingly comprehensive, no objects or relations in that world, and no faculty commensurate with it, however complex, can serve as a paradigm for ultimate knowledge. For Jain epistemology no mode of cognition will satisfy apart from total omniscience in the sense ascribed to it in the body of this paper.

NOTES

1. Joseph Needham, *Science and Civilisation in China* (Cambridge: Cambridge University Press, 1954–), III, p. 150.

2. Benjamin Nelson, "Sciences and Civilizations, 'East' and 'West,' Joseph Needham and Max Weber," *Boston Studies in the Philosophy of Science* II (1974):445–493.

3. The *Tathvarthadhigama Sutra* of Śri Umasvati was composed as early as the period of the oldest Jain commentaries and crystallizes an early and much respected epistemological tradition. Its date is given as 300 A. D. The commentary of Śri Pujyapada is the oldest extant commentary on the *Sutra* and accepted as definitive by the logician Sri Akalanka Deva in his *Rajavartika*. The *Sutra* together with the commentary will be taken as representative of the Jain epistemological literature. See Preface to *Tathvarthadhigama Sutra* of Śri Umasvati with the commentary of Sri Pujyapada translated by S. A. Jain (Calcutta: Vira Sasana Sangha, 1960). An exhaustive list of translations of the Sutra can be found in Karl Potter (ed.), *Encyclopedia of Indian Philosophies* Vol. I (Delhi: Institute for Indian Studies by Motilal Banarsidas, 1970). This essay follows the translation of S. A. Jain cited above.

4. I do not allege the absence of mathematical speculation during the formative period of Indian philosophy or afterwards since such an assertion is both contrary to fact and besides the point. I do not believe that the mathematical model does not provide the criteria governing the determination of truth in the Indian philosophical systems. Beyer in *A History of Mathematics* (John Wiley and Sons, 1968) writes that our notation for integers and an equivalent of the sine function in trigonometry are significant ancient Indian contributions (p. 237). However, there is a marked lack of continuity of tradition so that such events are sporadic (p. 229).

5. The non-living (ajiva) encompasses an elaborate structure including not only matter but time, space and motion among its elements. For general accounts see Surendrenath Dasgupta, *A History of Indian Philosophy*, Vol. I (Cambridge: Cambridge University Press, 1963), pp. 189–190 and pp. 195–198. Sarvepalli Radhakrishnan, *Indian Philosophy* (London: George Allen and Unwin, 1923), pp. 312-325. M. Hiriyanna, *Essentials of Indian Philosophy* (George Allen and Unwin, 1949), pp. 62 ff. and P. T. Rau, *The Philosophical Traditions of India* (London: George, Allen and Unwin, 1971). For detailed accounts see S. T. Stevenson, *The Heart of Jainism* (London: H. Milford, 1915), pp. 106 ff. Walter Schubring, *The Religion of the Jainas*, tr. by Amulachandra Sen and T. C. Burke (Calcutta: Sanskrit College, 1966), pp. 16-18. and Mohan Lal Mehta, *Outlines of Jaina Philosophy* (Bangalore: Jain Mission Society, 1954), pp. 26 ff.

6. The Jain doctrine of *anekanta* presumes that there is no privileged vantage point from which judgments may be made. All knowledge is relative to the standpoint of the observer: sense experience is only one of a variety of modes of experience. Jain epistemology holds that an object can be viewed from different points of view: existent, non-existent, one, many, identical, different, etc. Every object possesses indefinite attributes (dharmas) which are taken as actually existing in the object. When making a judgment the observer selects an aspect of the object. The term *Syat* is used to designate a particular point of view, i.e. from this aspect the object is such and not otherwise. For example, from the point of view of his father Anand is a son, but from the point of view of his brother he is a brother etc. The object itself is *anekanta*, a substratum which bears numerous characteristics.

Judgments regarding any object can be made in seven ways: Using the often cited clay pot as an example, perspectival judgments can be schematized as follows:

1. Relatively the pot exists.
2. Relatively the pot does not exist.
3. Relatively the pot does and does not exist (although not in the same respect).
4. Relatively the pot is indescribable.
5. Relatively the pot exists and is indescribable.
6. Relatively the pot does not exist and is indescribable.
7. Relatively the pot exists, does not exist and is indescribable.

Where the law of contradiction appears to be violated the conjunctive expression is to be taken as designated different standpoints from which each conjunct can be seen as true, i.e. true from that limited point of view. See Mohan Lal Mehta, *Outlines of Jaina Philosophy*, pp. 117 ff.

7. The Jain canons consider knowledge as divided into five categories: *abhinibodhika, sruta, avadhi, manahparyaya* and *kevala* (perception, scripture, clairvoyance, telepathy and total knowledge respectively). Two broad divisions are later added under which these five are subsumed: *pratyoksha* and *paraksha* (direct and indirect respectively). Perception is, in the *Tattvarthadhigama Sutra*, counted as indirect as is scriptural knowledge. See Mohan Lal Mehta, *Outlines of Jaina Philosophy*, pp. 85 ff. and Nathmal Tatia, *Studies in Jaina Philosophy* (Benares: Jain Cultural Research Society, 1951), Sanmati Publication number six, pp. 61–70.

8. The notion of what constitutes the mental realm is quite complicated in Indian systems. Suffice it to say that such functions as perceiving, deducing, willing, etc. are seen to be "mental" and belong to the materiality of the world as contradistinct from the power of spirit which cannot be reduced to mental acts. See Mohan Lal Mehta for the Jain application of this principle, p. 97.

9. See Norman Gulley, *Plato's Theory of Knowledge* (London: Methuen and Co. Lts., 1962), p. 48.

10. *Republic* VII, 526

11. *Republic* VI, 510.

12. See Nathmal Tatia, *Studies in Jaina Philosophy*, chapter IV, Mohan Lal Mehta, *Outlines of Jaina Philosophy*, chapter VI for detailed discussion of jain doctrine of karma. An older account can be found in Jagmanderlal Jaini, *Outlines of Jainism* (Cambridge University Press, 1916), pp. 26 ff.

13. *Republic* VII, 529.

14. Śri Pujyapada, *Sarvarthasiddhi*, p. 1 f.

15. Mailisena Syadvamanjari, *A Commentary on the Examination of the Thirty-two Stanzas of Hemacandra, XXIII*. For general accounts of this view see Dasgupta, *A History of Indian Philosophy*, Vol. I, pp. 179 f., and Radhakrishnan, *Indian Philosophy*, Vol. II, pp. 294 f. Bimal K. Matilal in *Epistemology, Logic and Grammar in Indian Philosophical Analysis* (The Hague: Mouton, 1971) contrasts the Jaina doctrine with that of the Advaitins and the Madhyamikas. The latter two regard the character of the phenomenal world as indeterminable: it is not a

merely fictive phenomenal realm but has a provisional existence, neither real nor unreal. Its character is logically indeterminable. For the Nyaya-Vaisesika any theory as to the character of phenomenality can be a valid theory concerning the character of the real: cause and effect are taken to be actual relations and the theory of causality a valid theory. The Madhyamika not only reject the validity of the claims of any theory of the phenomenal world but claim further that no theory concerning its character can be demonstrated. All such theories can be shown to be internally inconsistent. The Jaina takes a stand midway between these views arguing that each theory of the phenomenal world is consistent with a standpoint, but not absolutely valid. Thus if x is a particular theory of reality, given certain presuppositions from which x follows, an interpretation can be given to x such that x is true. For an account of the Jain doctrine of "tropes" or the acknowledgement of the validity of the positions of other Indian epistemological schools as partial views of the truth see P. T. Rau, *The Philosophical Traditions*, pp. 98 ff.

16. Since the mathematician may begin by studying sensible phenomena and then proceed to intelligible forms, the double interest results in a double function for mathematics: as propaedeutic to the knowledge of intelligible realities and as an instrument for describing and arranging the everyday world. See Robert Brumbaugh, *The Role of Mathematics in Plato's Dialectic* (Chicago: University of Chicago Libraries, 1942), p. 70.

17. I am indebted to Anders Wedberg, *Plato's Philosophy of Mathematics* (Stockholm: Almquist and Wiksell, 1955), p. 32 for this classification.

18. The Jain canons (See *Supra* note 9) do not change in the Sutra in this regard. The claim is made that this conception predates Lord Mahavira (the most recent founder and twenty-fourth *tirthankara* of Jainism).

19. Sri Pujyapada, *Sarvarthasiddhi*, p. 33.

20. Sri Pujyapada, pp. 34 ff.

21. *Meno.*

22. Norman Gulley, *Plato's Theory of Knowledge*, p. 28.

23. *Phaedo*, 75.

24. For the Pythagorean background of the physical representation of number see W. K. C. Guthrie, *A History of Greek Philosophy*, Vol. I (Cambridge: Cambridge University Press, 1962), pp. 242 ff. For the extent to which mathematical representation is said to characterize non-mathematical cases see Robert Brumbaugh, *Plato's Mathematical Imagination*.

25. See T. Heath, *A History of Greek Mathematics* Vol. 1. (Oxford University Press, 1921), p. 290; Anders Wedberg *Plato's Philosophy of Mathematics*, pp. 103 ff. and Richard Robinson, "Hypothesis in Plato," Gregory Vlastos (ed.), *Plato* (Doubleday, 1971), pp. 110 f. The position is summarized in Plato's *Republic* 511 thus:

> And when I speak of the other division of the intelligible, you will understand me to speak of that other sort of knowledge which reason herself attains by the power of dialectic, using the hypotheses, not as first principles, but only as hypotheses—that is to say, as steps and points of departure into a world which is above hypotheses, in order that she may soar beyond them to the first principles of the whole; and clinging to this and then to that which depends on this, by successive steps she descends again without the aid of any sensible objects, from ideas through ideas, and in ideas she ends.

26. Sri Pujyapada, *Sarvarthasiddhi*, p. 21.

27. This means only to apply to idea entities as ideal number but not to processes which in Jainism include action, time, space, motion, rest etc. See *Supra*, note 3.

28. The passages in *The Philebus*, 56c–59d and 61d–62b are interpreted by Wedberg as providing evidence for the accuracy of Aristotle's account in that they point to a separation between dialectic and philosophical arithmetic, the latter described as the study of numbers

which are not Ideas. These passages are also seen as pointing to eternal exemplars of geometrical Ideas. See Anders Wedberg, *Plato's Philosophy of Mathematics*.

29. Aristotle, *Metaphysics*, 1080 b, 11–14.

30. Aristotle, Metaphysics 1080 a, 30–33. See Leon Robin, *La theorie platonicienne des idées et des nombres*, p. 625. Anders Wedberg, *Plato's Philosophy of Mathematics*, pp. 116 ff.

31. Jacob Klein, *Greek Mathematical Thought and the Origins of Modern Algebra* (Cambridge: Massachusetts Institute of Technology Press, 1968), pp. 90 ff, and pp. 100 f. adds to this discussion by citing Aristotle's refutation of the Platonic view based on the mode of being Plato ascribes to mathematical objects (*Metaphysics*, 1076 a, 36 ff). Aristotle argues for the natural meaning of *arithmos*: "To be present in number is to be some number of a given object," (*Physics*, A 12, 22, 1b). Attributes such as white, round, etc., are arrived at by disregarding certain other attributes of a thing enabling one to extrapolate a quality apart from its contextual nexus. This quality can be predicated of other objects where, in turn, certain other qualities had been similarly disregarded. By subjecting the *aistheta* to this procedure, numerical aspects of being can be ascertained. Number is no longer subject to the senses, yet it does not have any independent ontological status. The mind tends to "think the mathematical objects which are not separate as if they were separate when it thinks them." (*De Anima*, 7, 431 b).

Part III
STUDIES IN
WESTERN CIVILIZATION

7. Thomas More and the Humanist Tradition: Martyrdom and Ambiguity

Charles Trinkaus

This paper, completed June 4, 1978, was originally presented to a symposium commemorating the 500th anniversary of the birth of Thomas More, and honoring the late Richard S. Sylvester, held in Washington, D. C., June 22, 1978. Since the paper's two main themes seek to affiliate Thomas More to the Renaissance humanist tradition by stressing the presence of a secular marytrology among the humanists and by emphasizing their awareness of ambiguity and complementarity in their conceptions of cultural and moral values, it seemed entirely appropriate to dedicate this paper to the memory of Benjamin Nelson, a man to whom I owe very much in the development of my own vision of history, culture, and morality. For Benjamin Nelson, though most certainly not playing the martyr, understood, better than most of our generation, the power and claims of past martyrdoms on the psychic life of all men. And he was deeply sensitive to the problematic character of the great themes of conscience and the cure of souls he illuminated so well in his studies of mankind's history.

This essay is an effort to pay tribute to a man of penetrating intellect, tireless devotion to his fellows, unyielding protection of his faith, and matchless sensitivity to the meaning of word and act. The collective tokens of contemporary admiration for More are manifold. Hardly one of us sees in him exactly what another has, but in all modern students of More there is a unanimity of respect and warmth of regard that responds to the relics of his life and mind as they reach to us across the centuries. We are a generation who in many senses has found in Thomas More the qualities we have missed in ourselves. We have made him embody our own ideals by the ways in which we have sought to interpret him, varied and clashing, yet ultimately agreeing. There was clearly something exceptional and large in him that could evoke such a unity out of plurality, such a coincidence of opposites.

It was my hope in trying to familiarize myself with some of the details of the magnificent Yale edition of the complete works of Thomas More that I might find something approaching an interpretive consensus developing, a consensus that clearly did not exist thirty years ago. But I have come gradually to conclude that however many the symposia, however many times scholars gather to exchange their thoughts and views of More, this will never be. Yet my humility before the scholarly and interpretive achievement of this past generation, both of the makers of the Yale edition and of the many others who have continued to be fascinated, study, and write, is vast, almost rivalling my humility before Thomas More himself. For this reason this paper will, for the most part, leave the discussion of More to others and retreat to a few observations on the humanist tradition from which he came, emphasizing two aspects of this tradition that can be identified in Thomas More. Somewhat arbitrarily, therefore, and yet with a strong conviction of their validity, I am going to offer two broader approaches than the usual academic conception of the humanistic tradition that seem relevant to this man: the presence of elements of martyrdom and of ambiguity in the tradition.

Martyrdom

Humanism, which is after all a term of our own modern invention, includes not only its meaning of admiration for and education in the ancient classics as first defined but comprehends the entire sweep of learning in the *studia humanitatis* of the Renaissance.[1] But far more than being a series of studies it was also a movement that, starting out from a scholarly and intellectual base, had a profound impact on the thought and action of that entire age.[2] Moreover, these Renaissance humanists who sought to influence their fellows of other professions and their secular and ecclesiastical rulers, also cheered themselves on and enlivened their onlookers and prospective listeners by reciting the lives and merits of the ancients. Petrarch with his *De viris illustribus* was only the first. The humanist tradition in a very literal (and literary) sense then was the rekindled memory of the great figures of the past who had sought somehow to bring their wisdom and learning to bear on the affairs of men. We shall, therefore, as a first broadening of our conception of a humanist tradition, review some of these ancient and early Christian figures with whom Renaissance humanists identified.

Ancient tradition itself was repeated by Cicero in his *Tusculans*, that "Socrates was the first who brought down philosophy from the heavens, placed it in the cities, introduced it into families, and obliged it to examine into life and morals, and good and evil."[3] In thinking of their own kind of learning as important in the lives of men, the Renaissance humanists always returned to this statement of Cicero's and others like it. Socrates, the martyr to the cause of the "examined life," is unquestionably evoked when we think of More, the martyr for his faith. But the connection of Socrates with More and humanism is deeper still. The "philosophy" that Cicero is talking about was that moral philosophy conceded with its qualities as the last of the *studia humanitatis*, and the term "philosophy" was used by Petrarch also to describe his own role of moral and cultural guidance. We are in fact engaged in a quarrel reaching over the centuries for the right to use that word, *philosophy*, and my remarks above show that it is still going on. But the quarrel over *philosophy* and *rhetoric* and the use of the words in a historically valid sense does indeed begin with Plato and his dispute with those who professed to teach wisdom, the *sophistai*. And it is at the end of his *Phaedrus*[4] in which Plato embraces so much of the rhetorical art that he has Socrates express his admiration for the young "rhetor," Isocrates, as the possible future "lover of wisdom" or "philosopher" who will combine the study of wisdom with the art and gift of speech. Similarly it was the mature Isocrates, the gifted and influential educator and advocate of Panhellenism, who spoke always of his philosophical rivals, Plato and Aristotle, as "sophists" and of himself and his friends as "philosophers." And again in the Renaissance the scholastics are charged with windy sophistry (*ventosa sophistica*), beginning with Petrarch, and including emphatic charges by Erasmus and our Thomas.

It was, then, a growing view among Renaissance humanists (Petrarch had not fully shared it, but Salutati certainly had) that the humanist tradition rightly began with Socrates, and who is to say they were wrong. But we, of course, know Socrates by no writings but only by Plato's and Xenophon's accounts, and other echoes which differ sufficiently for us to claim that we know him only by hearsay. Taking our hearsay from Plato, however, we might ask what sort of man Socrates was and whether he could be seen as a paradigm for Thomas More. The legend is good for our case if we accept, as Aristotle does,[5] that he was the true author of those ideas Plato presents as Socrates's in the *Republic*. And though we can agree with J. H. Hexter[6] that More's use of the *Republic* in *Utopia* was idiosyncratic and that his position was different from Plato's, I think we must also agree that the central question in both works was whether there can be any justice in our private dealings unless there is first justice in the structure of society as a whole. And if we come now to Plato's own views of justice there is the most fundamental disagreement between Plato and More: *justice* clearly meaning *equality* for More, (whether disguised as himself or as "Hythloday"), whereas Plato's definition for it was *proportion*. Moreover, another problem that deeply concerned More throughout his entire life was critical for Plato/Socrates as well: a concern basic to our notion of humanism, that of the role of the morally wise man in the affairs of the public and as a ruler of the state.

The story begins for Plato/Socrates, not in earlier but in different dialogues, namely the *Protagoras* and the *Theatetus*, where the sophist vision of man and moral behavior as represented by Protagoras is directly confronted by Socrates. We in our historical sophistication are inclined to follow Werner Jaeger[7] and Kristeller[8] and see in Protagoras (along with Gorgias and his pupil, Isocrates) the founders of a rival rhetorical tradition to Plato's and Socrates' philosophical one. But we can also see that, as viewed by another age, perhaps the two do not differ that much, and certainly in Renaissance humanist eyes they were differing not in their major purpose, which was to bring learning to bear on public affairs, but about the proper educational means. While Protagoras denies that any man can know other than what he senses and experiences, he also believes that man possesses an innate sense of justice and piety and can be taught to respect what his own society defines as justice. And here is the whole premise of the humanist tradition throughout its history—that most men can be taught to be virtuous, both the peasant and the king— whereas the Platonic/Socratic view is that God, not man, is the measure of all things and that only the philosopher who has achieved an insight into the divine form or structure of things can guide mankind toward justice, best of all when the philosopher himself is the king. And this is a higher (because cosmic) justice than that pragmatic human kind which is wrought in the law courts, taught in the classroom, or preached in the assembly. In this confrontation there are poignant problems for the Renaissance figures we know, be they humanists or other. But before we seek to untangle them we had better take a look at two other paradigms of humanism, better known to most in the Renaissance, Cicero and Seneca.

Let us remember that three of these figures—Socrates, Cicero, and Seneca—paid with their lives when the morality they so famously represented proved an obstacle to the ambition of rulers, and that the fourth, Plato, was deceived and misused by Dionysius, the tyrant of Syracuse. There was something in the Renaissance view (sharply expressed by More's "Hythloday") that a humanist would fare badly in the halls of power (however much he ought to be there). It is difficult to think of Cicero as a martyr because he has seemed in his private letters so manifestly crass and self-serving about his public career even though he

wanted it never to be forgotten that he had "saved the state." He brought
through his writings more of Greek rhetorical wisdom to the Latin West
than anyone but Quintilian, and certainly more of Greek philosophy than
anyone excepting only Boethius and Scotus Eriugena until the medieval
translations from Greek and Arabic and the Renaissance translations of
the Greek. But as one of the world's most renowned lawyers and orators,
and however ambivalent and vacillating he was in his devotion to political
action on behalf of public freedom and welfare, his contribution to the
moral and political thought of the Renaissance was ubiquitous. Justice for
Cicero came down to the fulfillment of a man's rationally projected roles
in the great society—as a participant in common humanity, as a member
of a nation, as a citizen of a city, and as an individual in a family. Although
Petrarch was able to misread Cicero as writing on behalf of retirement
from public affairs (as in his last days it was forced upon him),
Renaissance humanists more generally favored his forthright endorse-
ment of action and civic participation: "No man has any right to permit his
intellectual exercises to interfere with his performance of the duties of an
active life, for it is by its activity that virtue earns the highest praise. And
yet respites come frequently and bring with them abundant opportunities
for a return to study; moreover, the mind, which never rests, is quite
capable of keeping us, all unwitting, at the task of seeking knowledge."[9]

Cicero was an ancient humanist. With that no one has quarreled. But to
be so conceived, by both himself and by the humanists of the Renaissance,
his mastery of rhetoric (theoretical and practical) needed to be linked in
some way to philosophy. His allegiance to the practical realm over the
theoretical was plain enough. But did he profess philosophy only as a
prestigious adjunct to an effective rhetorical career, as some of his
statements suggest, or did he have a more genuine commitment? Jerrold
Seigel has stressed the importance of Cicero's philosophical side, but
seems to leave it, indeed, adjunctive, not genuinely integrated.[10] Cicero
does declare allegiance to the Academic school and sometimes takes over
the Stoic point of view as his own. He draws loosely and certainly
eclectically on a variety of sources. I believe his authentic position can be
reconstructed, something as follows: Religiously, he has no doubt
concerning the existence of phenomena that were beyond human
understanding, and he offered the traditional Roman ways of worshipping
and relating to religious reality his utmost reverence and care. He saw this
as something apart from philosophy, which he comprehended almost
entirely as the pursuit of wisdom in the conduct of human affairs. Natural
philosophy seemed useful but secondary to the study of ethics. A serious
man should be more careful not to commit himself to any one point of
view as the various schools and philosophers seemed to contradict

themselves and also to overlap and repeat too much. Hence Academicism in the end had the greatest appeal for him with its declaration that any formulation of truth could be matched by a contrary one, so that verisimilitude—probability—was the most for which one could hope. As a lawyer and an orator Cicero and others of similar profession would necessarily deal with a constantly fluctuating situation and a human constituency of the greatest variety. There the rhetorical commonplace, reaching a mixed audience, would indeed provide a basis for the only possible kind of loose unity of which the collective life of man was capable. But talent, practice of the art, experience, expanding knowledge leading to wisdom—all were essential. I believe that an image of Cicero as an orator and a philosopher such as this comes close to the way in which many Renaissance humanists read and judged him, and that this throws light on their own conceptions of their role in relation to philosophy. I believe also that behind Cicero's outlook was the serious grappling with the problem of collective wisdom and virtue by the Greek sophists, particularly Protagoras whom Plato respected sufficiently to confront in two different dialogues. Cicero also learned from the writings of Isocrates and from the rhetorical and moral works of Aristotle, but it is of especial interest that he actually translated Plato's *Protagoras*, a version that has been lost. I do not know if he ever quoted the *Theatetus*, but the point of view in the "Apology of Protagoras"[11] composed by Plato in this dialogue seems appropriate also to Cicero.

Until the fifteenth century Seneca was thought by some humanists to be a Nicodemite, or concealed Christian. And even as late as 1532 Lefèvre d'Étaples was still publishing a commentary on the forged correspondence between Seneca and St. Paul.[12] What Renaissance humanists saw in Seneca, some accepting and some doubting his Christianity, was the great moral counselor and guide to inwardness and tranquility in the face of life's disturbances and distractions. But Seneca also was a man of public affairs and a counselor of emperors. To many modern commentators his attitude has seemed ambiguous and problematic. In the end he committed suicide at Nero's order. Justice for this Stoic lay in the universal rational order of fate, *heimarmene,* and could be found only by resignation and acceptance. Yet he could counsel humanity and responsibility and offer highly practical psychological advice.

Seneca was important, especially in the early Renaissance, as the paradigm of the lay moral counselor. Petrarch modelled his figure of *Ratio* in the *De remediis* on the authentic Senecan *Epistulae ad Lucillium* as well as on the probably pseudo-Senecan *De remediis fortuitarum.* Seneca's influence on More seems to the outsider to be fairly limited. For instance, there are relatively few citations or allusions to him in *A Dialogue of Comfort.*[13] We shall see a reason for Seneca's diminishment presently.

We come to the interesting question of the extent to which the Church Fathers were regarded as predecessors by Renaissance humanists, and this involves the latters' attitudes toward the non-Christianity of their pagan models of wisdom—not a question to be hastily answered in a short paper. An answer can be approached only by examining the individual complexity found in the cases of each Renaissance writer, and I offer simply this observation: most Renaissance humanists were neither members of religious orders nor churchmen, or if they were, some, like Petrarch and Erasmus, did their best to live as laymen.[14] It was, perhaps, easier for them as laymen to identify with the non-Christian ancient humanist than with the venerable patristic figures who were in many instances saints. Yet Jerome and Augustine both attracted the interest of humanists powerfully and, to my reading, influenced a wide range of Renaissance humanists more deeply and persistently than the pagans. But again the differences of individuals is crucial. In the case of Augustine the Italian humanists played a major role in his late medieval and Renaissance rehabilitation prior to the Reformation. Because of Luther's and Calvin's overt Augustinianism a sectarian problem developed in the sixteenth century. But there were also influential Augustinians at least among the early Catholic Reformers.

For many of the humanists Augustine was the father who admired Plato and, even more significantly, one who became a philosopher on reading Cicero's *Hortensius*. I would not want to argue that the Ciceronian elements were stronger than the Platonic in the formation of Augustine's theology (he refutes and praises them both as the best of the pagans). In the *De doctrina Christiana* we have a more influential handbook on the use of lay learning, particularly the language arts and rhetoric, in the service of religion. Other fathers with whom Italian humanists closely identified were Lactantius and Jerome of course, and Eusebius, Basil, and Chrysostom among the Greeks. It should not be overlooked in late antiquity, both in the Latin and Greek worlds, how many men of rhetorical training, orators or *sophistai,* were converted and became Christian writers. Renaissance humanists gladly reported their examples and statements in support of classical studies and a more rhetorical theology. Since not all humanists were concerned with theology it was easier to admire the pastoral writings of the fathers and their pulpit oratory. Only as an interest in theology developed with Lorenzo Valla and the Florentine Platonists, and after them with Erasmus and other so-called Christian humanists of the North, did such philosophical theologians as Origen come to the fore. On the other hand, proponents of the powerful Renaissance theme of the dignity of man early found the theological base for their assertions in Augustine's emphasis on a human mental trinity mirroring the divine Trinity.

More's attachment to St. Augustine is well known, but as Father Surtz declared in his introductory section to the Yale translation of *Utopia*, the exact connection of *Utopia* with the *De civitate Dei* remains to be worked out.[15] Humanists such as Valla and Erasmus did not hesitate to polemicize with many of Augustine's positions. But it should never be forgotten that what were perhaps the pivotal issues of both the Renaissance and the Reformation had found their monumental exposition in the *De civitate Dei*, namely whether the world of man could be truly Christian and how much could mankind save itself from its own impulses to self-destruction apart from grace? Moreover book 19 of the *De civitate Dei* set the terms for the discussion of the great Erasmian-Morean problem of finding peace in a world where there was no peace. There were some who would have argued, not long ago, that to see the Church fathers as central to the thinking of the Renaissance was a contradiction in terms. But I cannot think that it is so anymore. Rather the Church fathers provided the frame within which Renaissance humanists in great preponderance viewed the antique past, explored the great pagan works in a new objectivity and depth, and were able to criticize them for their inappropriateness while admiring their historical actuality.

It would seem then that in speaking of the humanist tradition in the Renaissance we should recognize, as the Renaissance humanists did, that they had had their historical predecessors—seminal writers and thinkers of the classical and early Christian past whose intellectual and literary influence on all subsequent ages has been strong, but who had something special to offer the Renaissance. For the latter they offered examples of the possible social and cultural role of the man of learning, and powerful thinking concerning human nature and a just society. Some of them, at least, presented a model of a certain life-style: that of the intellectual who believed he could and should provide counsel and guidance to the mighty of this world, whether the emperor or the *demos*, only to arouse their ire in an especially vindictive way that could lead to execution, proscription, or commanded suicide. I would not want to suggest that here was the origin of the modern alienated intellectual any more than that Thomas More sought his own martyrdom. But the inner conviction of personal rightness ran strong in Socrates, at least as Plato represents him, as it also did in Cicero and Seneca. At the same time we have some evidence on which to question the absolute purity of motives of all of them. They were in certain respects antiheroes as well as heroes. But I would claim that for most of the individuals comprising the Renaissance phase of the humanist tradition, (though not many had the clean courage to risk and accept martyrdom), there was a sense of exclusion from the seats of power which they simultaneously coveted and despised. In Italy this was true even for those humanists who came from the leading families or the nobility. The motives of idealism—religious, moral, social—and those of self-advancement were never far apart nor totally distinguishable. When I think of the intelligence and integrity and confidence of More, I think of Coluccio Salutati and Lorenzo Valla and even Machiavelli more than of other Italians.

Ambiguity

I shall not try now to justify such an allegation of similarity of life-style between Renaissance and ancient humanists but wish to look at that other broad feature of the humanist tradition I proposed at the beginning of this essay. Thinking primarily of Italian humanist culture and its eventual influences upon a developing northern humanist culture, several inter-connected anthropological themes may be identified. Although I will make general statements concerning these themes, it should be understood that I would not wish it to be thought that all humanists engaged in speculation and argumentation concening these issues or that they always agreed. Indeed, they were frequently presented in dialogue as multi-sided controversy and debated between individuals. As themes they exhibit complementary positions rather than polarity, and are ordinarily seen as reflecting that exasperating humanist sense of ambiguity that still sets the teeth of scholarly dialecticians on edge.

The first such theme is the question of faith and knowledge, and of the right road toward acquisition of either: linguistic and historical studies or dialectic? From the perspective of purely intellectual history, here is the central issue between humanism and scholasticism, well elaborated in More's crucial letter to Dorp.[16] It is infrequently noticed that there was a certain agreement between most humanist critics of nominalism and their supposed enemies. Both rejected metaphysical realism. Both assumed the necessity of faith. Could one then speak about God and divine things? Both agreed that one could, provided such speech was seen to have a suppositious, "as if" status. What then was the issue? For the *nominales* of the *via moderna*, theology became the substitution of dialectical analysis of the terms used to speak about God in order to determine whether a logically consistent statement had been made for metaphysical speculation on the statement's correspondence to divine reality. The scriptures were to be accepted as the Word of God, but they were subject to the one grand nominalist assumption that God's power, barring violation of the law of contradiction, was absolute and He could do anything. What God actually did do, therefore, was not naturally necessary but contingent upon His will. What God had wrought and made known through scripture and nature had the authority of divine ordinance and the security of a divine covenant. It was theology's function to support what was divinely established within the world, not to determine its ultimate character by analogy to the science of nature.

For the humanist man could speak about God metaphorically, only as he imagined Him, and of invisible things only through the visible things of this world. But in this he had a model in Biblical poetics. Theology was necessarily poetic and concealed a higher truth behind its figures of speech, as did the scriptures. Such was the viewpoint of Petrarch, Boccaccio, and Salutati. To this was added the philological analysis of scripture by Valla and Manetti, followed later by Erasmus, based on the collation of Vulgate translation with Greek and Hebrew original. From it came a more literal acceptance of the bare scriptural meaning which sometimes had to be seen as concealing a mystery. Faith was a matter of trust and obedience and even more imaginative inspiration, and the resources of language were to be deployed by mankind for its mutual persuasion in joyous acceptance of divine mercy and truth.[17] It does seem clear, at least to this scholar, that an important element of reform was central to humanist religious reflection in its desire to circumvent the aridity and artificiality of a formalistic fidelity to church and sacraments, and to reinforce a necessary inwardness. Hence humanists led the way toward a reformation of letter into spirit which Protestants carried much farther, sometimes reverting to literalism, repudiating the authority of the historical church and changing the conception of sacrament. But it also seems clear that for earlier Italian humanism through to More and Erasmus, the aim was to restore authentic belief to Christian obedience and spiritual depth to the sacramental life, for both were part of the historical continuum and interpretive dialogue by which mankind collectively lived. Other and later humanists saw things in Protestant ways as well as also remaining Catholics. Ultimately, of course, it was the humanist way of dialogue and persuasion that failed in the violence of religious persecution and conflict.

The second complementary theme, which was also inherited from the scholastic past, was that of the relationship of intellect and will, reason and affect. Petrarch said, "It is better (*satius*) to love the good than to know the truth."[18] Will was inflamed and aroused by words. In his *De remediis*, on the other hand, *Ratio* is his spokesman. But *Ratio* did not speak in the syllogisms which he had ridiculed in his *Contra medicum*. It offered to *Gaudium* and *Dolor* pithy quotations, anecdotes from the classics, exhortations, all the arsenal of the rhetor's art. *Ratio* is really *Oratio* or Speech, and each chapter is the occasion for a humanistic sermon. It is, as the

Secretum and the *De otio religioso* reveal, man's affects that he is addressing, but in order to transform, not suppress them.

Behind will is power, as Salutati clearly saw. Theologically the debate over the primacy of the intellect or will, when it moved with Duns Scotus emphatically to the side of the will, reinforced the conception of God as a subjective power, as pure and absolute subjectivity, as He was perceived through the fourteenth century and on up through the Reformation. But correspondingly, human will meant human power; it was the faculty by which man asserted himself, either in obedience or living conformity to God or in defiance. What we see as the statist power dynamics of the age was already spelled out in the theology and political philosophy of the closing medieval centuries.

But could rhetoric, the humanist's reason, temper the fury of the affects? Salutati saw will as commanding and distorting the intellect. Valla saw man as all affect with virtue as *caritas* and *fortitudo*, vice as hate and cowardice. Prudence or malignity, faith or distrust, were merely intellectual instruments of the passions. Behind this debate, or rather sometimes fronting for it, was the question of grace and free will. It should be noted that the action and its moral character belonged to man, whether springing from free will or grace, human power or divine power. Power and love are linked in Franciscan theology and humanist psychology— fortitude and *caritas,* as Valla argued. Erasmus seemingly disagreed with Valla, who actually affirmed both free will and predestination leaving the reconciliation as a mystery beyond man. Luther seemingly agreed.

Action and contemplation, an ancient and medieval theme, acquires a new emphasis in the Renaissance. The speculative life was closest to that of the gods and the happiest for Aristotle. In the Middle Ages contemplation was often identified with the monastic way to salvation, but even more frequently contemplation was the way of the mystic. The old attitude lived on in Petrarch's connection of contemplation, meditation, and *otium* in his *De otio religioso* and in the *Secretum* and the *De vita solitaria.* But meditation has become a form of psychic concentration focusing on the last things. It draws the soul back together from its distraction by the trivial moments of daily experience. Already in the *De remediis* Petrarch praises action as a cure for melancholy, though the greater stress is upon attitudinal change brought on by contemplation. Meditation is ego-directed, not ego-exhausting; it is an internal dialogue, a focusing of rhetoric on the self.

Renaissance activism begins with Salutati's *De vita activa et operosa*, a work planned but never written. There is ample evidence of his views, however, in his letters and other writings. The value of activity is strongly affirmed by Leon Battista Alberti in the *Libri della famiglia* and again in *De iciarchia. Ozio* becomes the worst vice, even a sin, because God did not create man to live in idleness, but in order to employ his faculties. *Industria* is a leading virtue. For Valla, too, God was not quiescent but active and creative. So should be man, whose soul is not a *tabula rasa* painted by his sensations of the exterior world but a flame that casts its light and heat upon the world and uses it. In the emergent genre of "the dignity and excellence of man" Giannozo Manetti affirms that man's creation in the divine image and likeness is actualized by asserting his godlike qualities—beauty, intelligence, inventiveness, power, and opulence. Man's function is to understand and act—*intelligere et agere.* The Renaissance Platonists, Ficino and Pico, take this humanist vision of human activism and rebuild it into a Neoplatonic metaphysics, with especially Ficino stressing man's natural emulation of God. How much this emphasis is stressed in More is matter for discussion. It is certainly strongly projected in *Utopia* and is present in *A Dialogue of Comfort,* while, on the other hand, the question of a special Renaissance mode of meditation surely rises in the Tower works.

A fourth theme develops out of the others. It starts as the polarity of virtue and fortune but grows into a major new insight of the Renaissance. It might be called the "contextuality of character." Human free will is not only bathed in an aura of divine grace in the matter of justification but is both enfranchized and restricted by the social environment itself. The ideas of Machiavelli and More, likely the two greatest social thinkers to appear in the Renaissance, emerge from the earlier humanist discussions of this question and represent a break with the humanist tradition, if they do in fact break, because they aspire to go beyond.

The development begins, again, with that strangly neglected masterwork of Petrarch, *On the Remedies for Both Kinds of Fortune,* neglected since 1752 by us, that is, though widely copied, translated, printed, and read for the previous four centuries. There has been no printed edition in any language since then; moreover modern scholarly discussion, with a few recent exceptions, has been fragmentary. Petrarch's *Fortuna* turns out to be not simply a depiction of the unpredictable spinning of the wheel of chance but a panoramic overview of late medieval society and its typical life histories differentiated according to geographic, social, and cultural status. The countervailing virtues, as Heitmann[19] has shown, are intended as more effective prudential strategies for individual coping with the general exigencies of earthly life than the depressed shuddering and elated shouting that character-shaping circumstances too often evoke. If Petrarch was a Pelagian, it was in this realm of moral behavior; grace, he also thought, was essential for salvation. But the achievement of a degree of moral autonomy was an inescapable precondition for the trusting acceptance of the creation which might allow an infusion of grace. The parallel question, which Hexter[20] has raised concerning the Utopians, was whether More saw them as more grace-worthy than Christian Europeans of his day. Hexter said "Yes," and I am inclined to agree, but must leave it to the Moreans.

Lorenzo Valla, suspicious not only of the Pelagians of his day, especially the *nominales*, but also of the humanists too enamored of Stoicism (including Petrarch), would have demurred. As in the *Utopia* later, Valla's *De voluptate* or *De vero falsoque bono* declares itself an irony and discusses through the *personae* of some contemporary humanists what a "natural," i.e., pre-Christian morality would be like. Valla's Epicurean, who has no knowledge of Christ, is presented in terms of individual psychology and morality. He is not embedded in a carefully devised economic and social structure as in the case of More, nor in a political structure, as in Machiavelli's case. Epicurean man lives as his everyday experience dictates his needs and not according to abstract moral formulas as did Stoic man. Virtue, or the qualification and specification of motivation and behavior, grows out of experience and the social environment. But virtue is affect, and a form of object-oriented love. Pre-Christian man's love is self-directed or family-directed and pleasure-determined as in the case of animals. Natural man is not different from the animals except for variations in intellectual and emotional powers. Only with Christ does mankind transcend the animal kingdom with man's gift of immortality of soul. Christian man has transferred his love to Christ and seeks his pleasure in beatification. In fact, "pleasure," "charity," "love," and "beatification" are no more than contextually differentiated words meaning the same thing. Just as affect is human emotional power, language is man's intellectual power, and is qualified and differentiated in the active give-and-take of existence.

Giovanni Gioviano Pontano carries the analysis farther still. A major portion of his writings was devoted to a detailed analysis of the socially contextual character of the virtues. He saw these in terms of linguistic usage which he derived from observing self-motivation and the behavior of others. In his *De sermone,*[21] or *On Speech,* he develops a *logos* doctrine for everyday social intercourse, just as Erasmus, following Valla, insisted that Greek New Testament *logos* should be translated as *sermo* not *verbum*—Christ in His entire life and His sayings of the gospels as the "speech" of God.[22] What Valla and Erasmus sought to make sacred was left secular by Pontano, though he was not at all unaware of its religious implications. Declaring that *De sermone* was a study of the rhetoric of daily human relations, comparable to the more formal and traditional rhetoric of the law court and assembly, Pontano analyzes such positive qualities as *comitas, facetitas, humanitas*—affability or courtesy, merriment or wittiness, gentility or kindness—as character types that he designated by adjectival nouns: *comis, facetus, humanus.* Such men are essential to the well-being of society and make earthly life pleasant, joyful, and bearable. Notable is his use of "humanity" not merely as higher culture but closer to our use of it in a philanthropic sense, contrary to Aulus Gellius's declaration. Equally essential to holding society together in mutual concord and trust are veracity and the truthful man. On the other side are the social vices and evil character types, brilliantly and savagely depicted by Pontano. Pontano combined his studies of classical literary and moral works with his experience as counselor and chancellor in the Neapolitan court and diplomatic service, and there is an important parallelism of career between Pontano and More as well as a carry-over of insight.

Pontano is regarded as an important immediate predecessor to Machiavelli in his social and historical realism. Other humanists such as Alberti, Poggio, and Valla have also been signaled in a more fragmentary sense for this "honor." I will not enter into the hazardous debate as to whether Machiavelli was a humanist (though I would argue he was one). Also, Hexter has made the classical comparison of Machiavelli and More.[23] But I do have a single point to make, which I share with Hexter. Machiavelli's realism (so-called) was not only a realism of external observation but a realism of rhetoric and advocacy. He wanted to change things by showing princes and statesman how to behave in order not to be entrapped in the concatenation of circumstances that was called "fortune" but was in actuality what we would call the political structure and history. But here I would recall that the most serious problem for Machiavelli (apart from the lack of a militia or some other effective organization for war), and one leading to political failure and/or social disaster, was that men's characters were formed by their experience, so that when circumstances changed, they themselves did not change. Machiavelli's recommendations, though admired by many, can also seem in some ways as paltry and certainly ineffective. He advocated forceful, determined, even impulsive action, on the basis of at least some calculation of the structurally determined balance of forces and some sense of ancient and modern precedents for success and failure. As More and Erasmus knew, princes and rulers were already behaving this way and, as we know, they still are today. To what avail?

More well knew the limits of political action and power even in achieving its only possible goal, the retention or expansion of power. And he knew the human consequences of this system well, even though, whether fatuously or not we cannot say, he lent himself to it. In his *Utopia* More set up the classical issues over which good men have differed since then, especially that of the intellectuals and the humanists participating in power (only to then illustrate both sides of the argument in his own life). More also, (and here I agree with Hexter),[24] saw in property the root of all evil, or perhaps more accurately, the root of all sin, and he devised his Utopian communism as a mental experiment outlining an alternative. He did this in all seriousness and not simply to show how a people who had never heard of Christ were more Christian than Christians. As again Hexter insists, he was thinking of his own world and its problems. Nor was he totally naive about the consequences, costs, and problems of such a solution, imaginatively creating fully totalitarian and authoritarian institutions for its maintenance.

If, however, More was actually proposing Utopian communism as a programmatic solution, he would have departed from the humanist tradition. I believe he did see the problematic character of his solution; through his character of "Morus," he genuinely expressed rejection of it at the end of the dialogue. He saw even more clearly and dramatically the tragedy of the opposite failure of mankind to rise above its institutions because he lived with them and directly observed the consequences. In possessing this double vision, More preserved the essential dialogic ambiguity of the humanist tradition.

NOTES

1. See Paul Oscar Kristeller's basic statement, his "Humanism and Scholasticism in the Italian Renaissance," Byzantion XVII (1944–45):346–74, reprinted in his Studies in Renaissance Thought and Letters (Rome, 1956), pp. 553–83 and in his Renaissance Thought, the Classic, Scholastic and Humanist Strains (New York, 1961), pp. 92–119, reasserted and elaborated in a sequel of other writings.

2. See Eugenio Garin, Der italienische Humanismus (Bern, 1947) Eng. trans. by Peter Munz (Oxford and New York, 1965).

3. Tusc. V, iv.

4. Phdr. 278c–279a.

5. Aristotle cites Socrates in all references to the Republic in his Politics.

6. The Complete Works of Thomas More (hereafter CW) IV, Utopia, ed. by Edward Surtz, S. J. and J. H. Hexter, Introduction, cix–cx. And see especially Hexter's comments, cvi–cviii.

7. Paideia: the Ideals of Greek Culture, Vol. I (New York, 1945), pp. 298–321.

8. Renaissance Thought, pp. 11–12.

9. De officiis, I, 6.

10. Rhetoric and Philosophy in Renaissance Humanism, The Union of Eloquence and Wisdom (Princeton, 1968), esp. pp. 11–18.

11. Tht. 166a–168b.

12. See Letizia A. Panizza, "Gasparino Barzizza's Commentaries on Seneca's Letters," *Traditio* XXXIII (1977):297–341 for a survey of humanist conceptions of Seneca. For Lefèvre d'Étaples, p. 339.

13. *CW* XII, Index s.v. Seneca. Clearly, however, More was saturated with Stoic notions, whatever their provenance.

14. On the other hand, the number of ecclesiastics involved with humanism was remarkable. See Kristeller's "The Contribution of Religious Orders to Renaissance Thought and Learning," *The American Benedictine Review*, XXI (1970):1–55 and esp. Appendix B, "Humanists and Scholars of the Religious Orders."

15. *CW* IV, clxvi.

16. *The Correspondence of Sir Thomas More*, ed. by Elizabeth F. Rogers (Princeton, 1947), letter 15, 17–74. See Salvatore I. Camporeale's study of the possible influence of Lorenzo Valla on More, finding at least extensive parallels of position between the Letter to Dorp and certain texts by Valla, *Da Lorenzo Valla a Tommaso Moro, Lo Statuto Umanistico della Teologia* (Pistoia, 1973), *Memorie Domenicane*, n. 4.

17. See the quotation from Coluccio Salutati in my *In Our Image and Likeness* (London, 1970), pp. 62–63.

18. Francesco Petrarca, *Prose*, ed. by G. Martellotti *et al.* (Milan/Naples, 1955), p. 748.

19. Klaus Heitmann, *Fortuna und Virtus, Eine Studie zu Petrarcas Lebensweisheit* (Köln/Graz, 1958), II. "Fortuna und Virtus in der Auseinandersetzung."

20. *CW* IV, lxxiv–v *et seq. et passim.* I take it Hexter does say, "yes," in his paragraph lxxvi–lxxvii.

21. *Ioannis Ioviani Pontani de sermone libri sex*, ed. by S. Lupi and A. Riscato (Lugano/Padua, 1954).

22. See Marjorie O'Rourke Boyle, *Erasmus on Language and Method in Theology* (Toronto and Buffalo, 1977), esp. c. 1, "Sermo" and c. 2, "Oratio."

23. *The Vision of Politics on the Eve of the Reformation* (New York, 1973), chap. 4.

24. *CW* IV, cv–cxxiv, "The Radicalism of *Utopia*."

8. German Idealism in a Comparative Perspective: Hierarchy in the Thought of Fichte

Louis Dumont

From the time we first met in 1971, Benjamin Nelson greatly encouraged my comparative efforts. As a modest tribute to his memory, here is an extract from a work in progress dealing with social philosophy in Germany between 1770 and 1830.

The enterprise is comparative in two senses, or rather on two levels. First it draws its basic categories from a previous study of Indian society and culture, that belonged technically to social anthropology, and second it focuses on the different forms that the modern system of ideas and values has actually taken in different countries, the national variants, as I call them, of modern ideology. In the former work, the comparative aspect implicit in social anthropology has been made explicit and has resulted in two pairs of oppositions bearing on values: hierarchy v. equality on the one hand, and on the other holism v. individualism, or the paramount valuation either of the social whole or of the human individual. In the present case those two distinctions are brought to bear on the interpretation of German social ideology as compared to its French counterpart.

To allow for some development, an earlier paper has been split into two: while elsewhere I deal with the Franco-German contrast in relation to the conception of the nation, here I shall concentrate on some aspects of Fichte's thought.[1]

The social and political philosophy of Fichte still poses a problem today. Fichte explicitly set out to be the philosopher of the French Revolution. And yet he has often been considered in Germany, notably by the historian Meinecke writing before the first world war, as a precursor of pangermanism or of the theory which binds the state to the collective will-to-power of a people. On the other hand, the French philosopher, who has given a painstaking exegesis of Fichte's system, Martial Guéroult, has been deeply concerned with showing that Fichte throughout his life and writings remained perfectly faithful to the Revolution and that whatever else is found in Fichte on that level is quite secondary, whether it be his deeply German manner of thinking and feeling or his "German messianism," not to speak of the misunderstandings and falsifications or misrepresentations he has been made to suffer under.[2] In the face of such conflicting opinions, I should like to show that we can better account for the social philosophy of Fichte and for its subsequent destinies by starting from the difference between the two sub-cultures, German and French. I shall mainly endeavour to show the presence in Fichte, decidedly equalitarian though he is, of a hierarchical form of thought the equivalent of which it would be difficult to detect among the French revolutionaries.

Let us go straight to the heart of the difficulty, the *Addresses* to the German Nation—those lectures delivered by Fichte after the Prussian defeat at Iena in Berlin then occupied by Napoleon's troops. From the divergent interpretations and contradictory valuations of our two witnesses we can extract a minimum of agreement. For Guéroult, Fichte remains true to the revolutionary ideal, while according to Meinecke Fichte goes one step forward—but only one step—towards the truly German, more or less pangermanist, conception of the state. We observe that both are actually agreed on one point: that there is a universalist component in Fichte's thought (which Guéroult praises while Meinecke deplores it). Let us take this common admission as our point of departure. We shall even admit with Guéroult that this universalism is the essential or encompassing component in the *Addresses* and in Fichte's social thought in general. Yet it does not account by itself for the exaltation of the German nation, which is the more striking as the latter was in fact—unlike Prussia—absolutely non existent in those days. We are thus bound to search for another element that combines with Fichte's universalism to produce his nationalism.

There are two lineages in German thought. As against the Herderian, or one might say historicist or monadic lineage, which has as its basic tenet the specificity and irreplaceability of each culture or people, Fichte belongs with Kant and even with Hegel to the universalist lineage. Meinecke can reproach him for extolling in the last analysis not the concrete nation as a particular corporate will-to-live, but the "nation de raison," the nation as a rational universal entity. Of course it is true that the universalist or cosmopolitic ideology does not bar patriotism, the French *levée en masse* in 1793 seems to bear witness to the fact, and it is easily understood: if I conceive of myself as an Individual, a representative of the human species, I nevertheless live in fact in a given society or nation, and I spontaneously look at this more restricted circle as the empirical form that the human species takes for me, so that I may feel an attachment for it without justifying my feeling explicitly through what differentiates my nation from others. Yet this is not enough in Fichte's case. His stance is something like "the German spirit is characterized by universality," on the face of it a quite ambiguous statement.

The devoted French biographer of Fichte, Xavier Léon, has shown that, in the *Addresses* and other texts of the same period, Fichte put forth theses bearing a certain likeness to those of Romantics like August Wilhelm Schlegel and Schelling. On the present issue, Fichte admits with Schlegel that the German people is destined to dominate the world, but he thoroughly modifies the meaning of the assertion by basing it on the identity of universality and germanity, a trait which was, by the way, already present in his slightly anterior Patriotic Dialogues.[3] It is all essentially a matter of humanity and its development. The ambiguity lies in the fact that, when Fichte insists on the regenerative function of the German people, and on the resulting attribution of precedence to Germany, we do not know whether he is unilaterally applying universalism to a particular population, as by a sort of hypertrophied patriotism, or whether he is asserting the hegemony of a will-to-live that uses universalism merely as a prop. Actually, if we want to remain close to Fichte's thought, we must maintain that for him the two aspects do not exclude each other as they do for his interpreters, but coincide. This coincidence is the fact that, strange as it looks, we must try to understand.

As already stated, Fichte is on the whole a stranger to the Herderian and romantic notion of the diverse characters of cultures or peoples as so many facets of the richness of the universal Whole. When he does use this notion in a passage of the thirteenth address, it is part of a clever argument directed precisely against the romantic dream of a new Christian-Germanic Empire. More generally, it is true that Fichte adopts in that period the current stereotypes of the excellence of the German character, of the German language, etc. . . . , but he does so essentially in order to state a *hierarchy* among peoples *in the name of the very values of universalism*. Now I contend that, apart from any borrowing from the Romantics, it is possible to show the presence in Fichte's thought in general, alongside of a strong individualistic-cum-universalistic stress, of a holistic aspect and more especially of a hierarchical component. I shall leave out here the holistic tendency, very strong in the authoritarian socialism of the *Closed Commercial State*, and which could be found also in passages of other texts—uneasily cohabiting with individualistic features, but this is after all an ubiquitous trait in modern thought, including sociological thought.[4] What is more noteworthy is the emergence, all along the works of Fichte, and in clear contrast with the Enlightenment and French revolutionary thinking, of a hierarchical form of thought.

To demonstrate this presence of hierarchy in Fichte's thought, I must first recall the definition of hierarchy to which the previous study mentioned above has led me.[5] I shall briefly note a few fundamental points: 1) Hierarchy has in principle nothing to do with political power although it is often found inextricably enmeshed in it. 2) Nor does hierarchy require a linear succession of terms or entities, although it can generate such chains. 3) It is most economically seen as a relation between *two* entities in which the one is super-, the other subordinated. The relation of the two entities to a whole being explicitly or implicitly present, the most immediate case is when the first entity constitutes the *whole* in question while the second is *an element* of it (system and subsystem). 4) The hierarchical relation is best analysed into two statements bearing on two ranked levels: on the superior level the two ranked entities are identical, or consubstantial, on the inferior level they are opposed as contrary, complementary or contradictory. Therefore I speak of the hierarchical relation as the *encompassing of the contrary*. Thus in the creation of man and woman in the first Book of Genesis, Eve is fashioned from a rib of Adam to signify that woman is encompassed in man, man being: a) on the first level the representative of the human species as a whole; b) on the second level the opposite of woman. Apart from the linguistic fact of man (or Adam) figuring on the two levels, the essential feature is that *the couple as as whole hierarchizes its components*, or in other words unites them while recognizing their difference.

Fichte is fiercely equalitarian on the political level, in contrast with Kant and with most of the Germans—but in agreement with Herder (and Rousseau)—and in perfect consonance with the French Revolution in its Jacobin development. Is it not therefore surprising to find an example of formalized hierarchy in the very book that the young Fichte devotes in 1793 to the defense of the Revolution, the *Contributions to the rectification of the judgement of the public*? A single diagram is found in the book. It is intended to show the State as subordinated to the individual. It shows four concentric circles of which the largest includes—or in my language encompasses—the second, and so on: the "domain of consciousness," i.e., individualism in its moral form, embraces the domain of natural law, the latter in turn that of contracts in general, and this last that of civil contract or of the State. Here is, repeated thrice, precisely the encompassing disposition through which I have defined hierarchy.[6] It is remarkable that this argument is found in a vindication of the French Revolution against the attacks of Burke and Rehberg. Of course there is no conflict at all between this schema and Fichte's purpose, for it deals with pure hierarchy, which has nothing to do with (political) power. Yet, it is paradoxical that a staunch equalitarian should resort to a form of pure hierarchical thought. I bet that one would be hard put to find anything similar in contemporary revolutionary France. Already at such an early date, Fichte presents, alongside of the equalitarian conviction through which he is in communion with the Revolution, a quite different form of thought.

There is an element of social hierarchy in a passage of the *Closed Commercial State* where the needs of the several social categories are carefully distinguished. The scholar or scientist, in the interest of what we could call the output of his work, needs rich foods and a refined environment while, at the other end of the social scale, the peasant is able to assimilate coarse meals, which are sufficient for him. The trait is interesting in contrast to the stress on the equalitarian principle in the book at large, and still more so in contrast to the French developments in the direction of a state regulated economy, to which Fichte's model is parallel.[7]

The examples of hierarchy I just referred to are yet details, local, almost anecdotic occurrences. Far more weighty, decisive indeed in my view, is the presence of the hierarchical opposition at the very heart of Fichte's system of philosophy, in that dialectic of the "I" (or self) and the "Not-I" (not-self) which constitutes the foundation of his *Wissenschaftslehre* (1794), the "transcendental dialectic," as Philonenko calls it, that establishes the conditions of all knowledge. The demonstration lies at hand, for it is the "I" that posits the "not-I." As in the case of Adam and Eve, there are two levels in the relationship: on the first level, the I or self is undifferentiated, it is the absolute I or self; on the second level, the self posits within itself the not-self, and *ipso-facto* posits itself as against the not-self, so that we have, facing each other, the self and the not-self. The not-self is on the one hand contained within the self, on the other hand it is the opposite of self. This strictly hierarchical disposition of the Fichtean dialectic is noteworthy from many angles, especially perhaps with regard to Kant and to Hegel. On the one hand it is the hierarchical disposition that allows Fichte to integrate into a whole Kant's two Reasons, pure Reason and practical Reason. On the other hand, Hegel's dialectic will be no more hierarchical.

The fact takes some wonder and is worth pondering, for the young Hegel was intent on totality and had finally reached a hierarchical definition of it when he wrote, in his last fragment in Frankfort, that Life was "the union of union and nonunion" (*Verbindung und Nichtverbindung*).[8] Here is, if anywhere, that "encompassing of the contrary" through which I proposed to define hierarchy.

This formula of the young Hegel is no *obiter dictum*. It is central to what has been called by the Editor the "Fragment of a system," a text that, even grievously incomplete as we have it, marks the conclusion of the whole period of the "early theological writings" and is roughly contemporary with Hegel's resolve to join Schelling in Iena and enter the career of philosophy proper. The importance of the formula is confirmed from the fact that we can follow it up in subsequent writings. In Iena it is identity that must be conceived as "the identity of identity and non-identity," and in the *Logic* we find the infinite as the union of the infinite and the finite.[9]

Yet there is no gainsaying the fact that this unmistakable hierarchical aspect is eliminated from Hegel's definitive thought. What has happened? It is certainly not the case that Hegel has turned his back to the motto in which he had condensed the yearnings of his youth. Rather a gradual transformation took place, that is signalled, in Iena and later on, by changes in vocabulary indicative of conceptual modifications and shifts. The totality that was called Life in the "Fragment" became the Absolute, and then the absolute Spirit, that is to say the Absolute as subject. All this is well known, but, as the hierarchical perception itself, so its fate has not hitherto attracted notice.[10]

What became of it can most graphically and economically be seen from the section of the *Logic* that deals with the dialectic of the infinite and the finite, to which a recent exegete attributes a central place and exemplary value.[11] In this long and toilsome discussion, a real *Auseinandersetzung*, Hegel asserts not only, as hinted at above, that the infinite contains the finite, but also conversely that the finite contains the infinite. The reader who admits that the latter statement is obviously not true *in the same sense* as the former, who bears in mind our remarks, and who immerses himself in the intricacies of the development will I think conclude as I do that Hegel here labours very hard to eliminate the dissymmetry inherent in the relationship and give equal status to its two poles. Infinity, which attached, to begin with, to the encompassing of the contrary, will in the end have been transferred to the *process* of transition from one pole to the other, and to *negativity* as the motive force or principle of this process.[12] All in all, infinity has transited—whether wholly or only partly—from the domain of wholeness or transcendance to that of immanence and dialectics. It seems that Hegel's effort, or a considerable part of it, was precisely directed at the elimination of the hierarchical aspect, and judging from this particular form of it, his dialectic is likely to owe to this intention a good deal of its complexity.

Of course this is not to say that hierarchical aspects cannot be detected in Hegel's system as a whole, and especially in the architectonics of it. It reappears explicitly, or almost so, at the supreme level, that of Absolute Spirit,[13] and implicitly, almost shamefacedly, at less exalted levels, at any rate in the social philosophy (Objective Spirit), for it is clear that Hegel's State, as holistic, encompasses in our sense of the term civil society and its individualism. We cannot here enlarge on those aspects and must be content with stating that hierarchy, although implicitly present at the start, has been somewhat forcibly expelled from the core of Hegel's philosophy—an event of tremendous impact if one thinks of his posterity. Everything looks as if Hegel had sensed in his own thinking the incongruity that we detected in Fichte's *Contributions*, and eliminated it. With Hegel the equalitarian value has grown more ambitious and exclusive. So to speak, the acculturation to the French Revolution has gone one wide step deeper. To highlight this point was the intention of this brief Hegelian excursus.

Let us return to Fichte. We saw that, from the *Contributions* of 1793 to the *Addresses* of 1807–8, including the transcendental fulcrum of the *Wissenschaftslehre*, a hierarchical component is found in Fichte. We are now in a position to answer the question we asked about the *Addresses* at the beginning: what, aside from any occasional borrowing from the Romantics, Fichte has added to the universalistic individualism of the French Revolution is precisely this deep hierarchical perception. It takes no wonder that for Fichte one particular people, opposed to other peoples as the self is opposed to the not-self, embodies humanity at a particular time. It embodies, that is, the human self as a whole. This is how Fichte may at this point join the predominant current of German thought, and the Romantics in particular.

At this point, it is apposite that we should try and see more precisely the relation between Fichte's thought and the German ideological pattern in general. There is a powerful holistic trend in German ideology at large, and in conjunction with it we may I think admit that, as is commonly held by foreigners and not by them alone, the German people as a whole were, in our period and beyond it, strongly inclined to obey the powers that be. Admittedly, this is a stereotype, but for the present purpose we shall take the statement as true in comparison with other west European peoples and the French in particular. In agreement with this general background, German intellectuals in their great majority admitted the necessity of subordination in society. Thus, according to Kant, man is an animal that, in society, needs a master. Now what is true within the society is true, *mutatis mutandis*, outside it, and given a plurality of nations it was only natural, from such a point of view, to believe that some of them should dominate the others. Combined with the ethnocentrism or sociocentrism which is found universally—the valuation of "we" as against "others," the strangers—we have here the social basis of what has been called "pangermanism."

In this environment, there were few champions of equalitarianism among thinkers of influence, but they were determined. Herder and Fichte, both of lowly origin and dependent on the affluent in their youth, hated the domination of man over man. It is remarkable that they were nevertheless able to think in hierarchical terms, for it means that they spontaneously disentangled hierarchy—essentially a matter of values—from political (and economic) power. The two things are most generally confused, as we know only too well. On this point the contrast with Rousseau, whose insertion in society was very similar but whose social milieu was different, seems decisive. Thus, the fact that the thought of the staunchly equalitarian Fichte was as essentially hierarchical as we have shown is an index of the strength of the holistic component in German culture.

We can now see clearly how insufficient it is to consider him either as a faithful follower of the French Revolution who would have been only secondarily endowed with German characteristics, or as a precursor of pangermanism unable to rid himself completely of the abstract universalism of the French. If one may extend the use of the word "translation" from the linguistic to the cultural domain, then one will say that Fichte has translated the French Revolution into German. A convinced equalitarian, he did not admit of subordination in society as grounded in the nature of man, and at the same time he kept alive a strong sense of hierarchy, indeed he was able to give hierarchy a philosophical form, albeit indirectly. Moreover, as Herder before him, he applied modern individualism on the collective level, making of the people or nation an individual of a superior order, and again as Herder, he saw humanity as embodying itself in modern times in the Germanic culture-people, or the German nation.[14]

Perhaps a little more can be said in this place about hierarchy and German ideology. If there is some truth in the stereotype that represents the German people, in contrast for instance to the French in the same period, as having a propensity to obey, if it is true that in German thought, again in contrast to others, the necessity of subordination in society is more often admitted then denied, then we would expect some of the great German philosophers who have dealt at least occasionally with the problems of society to have searched for the values that might justify subordination, and, just as I have been led to do by the exemplary Indian case, to have isolated explicitly hierarchy as distinct from, if combined with, power. This is not the case. At any rate the whole of German idealist social philosophy can be, and has often been, surveyed without mentioning at all hierarchy proper. How can this fact be understood? A first answer is obvious: as we have seen from what happened with Hegel, those philosophers have worked under the spell of the Reformation and, more immediately, of the French Revolution, and they were more oriented towards the powerful contemporary individualist and equalitarian trend than towards the plain elucidation of their own social make-up.

But after all our question is wrongly put, witness the hitherto unsuspected but glaring presence of the hierarchical form of thought at the core of Fichte's philosophizing. True, Fichte does not directly name what I called the hierarchical opposition, but he does spontaneously set it to work, and thus he virtually uses the distinction between hierarchy and power. Only the point is not acknowledged, not "thematized." And we can well fancy why it is not. Fichte's equalitarianism was limited to the refusal of subordination in society; it did not prevent him—perhaps it did not *yet* prevent him—to hierarchize ideas, but for this to be possible the two domains had to remain separate. In other words, Fichte could not possibly recognize the encompassing form of thought as hierarchy, that is as something that, although distinct in principle, is nevertheless present in combination—lawfully even if not factually—in social subordination. Fichte's achievement is remarkable, if one compares it with the young Hegel's confounding under the category of "domination" (*Herrschen*) despotic power, the transcendence of God among the ancient Jews and that of the Kantian imperative.[15] It may be that Fichte had reached the limit which no human mind could transcend under the circumstances, that is, at a time when an all-powerful equalitarian ideal inspired minds of his sort.

Here is perhaps a fateful turn of history. For let us allow ourselves a wishful reconstruction: let us suppose that Fichte or another thinker had crossed the limit and clearly distinguished hierarchy from power, and that this acquisition had, in time, slowly permeated common German consciousness. Then the German people, predisposed as it was to accept subordination, would have learnt to distinguish between factual power and its legitimacy with reference to values, and the Germans could have avoided plunging into the outrageous and apocalyptic masquarade that we have lived through and that has left its scar on them as well as on us.

NOTES

1. The complementary paper, referred to hereafter as "Aspects," is "Aspects of Interaction Between Cultures: Herder's Volk and Fichte's Nation," in Joseph B. Maier and Chaim I. Waxman, eds., *Ethnicity, Identity and History: Essays in Memory of Werner J. Cahnman* (Transaction Books, 1982). The earlier paper was read at the 8th Annual Meeting of the *International Society for the Comparative Study of Civilizations*, Northbridge, California, March, 1979. The original version, unpublished in French, "The Social Philosophy of German Idealism," has appeared in English translation, not seen by the author: "Communications Between Cultures," in, *Discoveries, Third International Symposium*, Paris, October, 1978, ed. by Bruce M. Adkins (Tokoya: Honda Foundation, 1979), pp. 87–113. A French summary has appeared in *Libre* 6:233–250.

2. Martial Guéroult, *Etudes sur Fichte* (Paris, 1974), pp. 142–246, originally in *Revue philosophique*, 64e année, vol. 128 (1939), pp. 226–320. Friedrich Meinecke, *Weltbürgertum und Nationalstaat*, 3tte Ausgabe, (München, 1915), pp. 96–125.

5. Xavier Léon, *Fichte et son temps*, 2 books in 3 vol. (Paris, ed. 1954–9), II-1, pp. 433–63; II-2, pp. 34–93.

4. Cf. for the Durkheimians my *Homo Hierarchicus*, note 3a; also "The anthropological community and the ideology," *Social Science Information*, 18–6 (1979). Closer to our topic, Karl Pribram, in a seminal paper published in 1922 and that has a prophetic ring, has called "pseudo-universalism" (pseudo-holism) the underlying ideological formula that he showed to be common to Prussian nationalism and to Marxian socialism: "Deutscher Nationalismus und deutscher Sozialismus," *Archiv für Sozialwissenschaft und Sozialpolitik*, 49 (1922):298–376.

5. The following is taken *verbatim* from "Aspects." Cf. *Homo Hierarchicus* (coll. Tell, 1979), pp. 396–403 and from "The Anthropological Community and the Ideology."

6. J. G. Fichte, *Sämmtliche Werke*, 1845, Vol. VI, pp. 39–288; the figure is on page 133. The reader might think that Fichte's circles, or some of them, indicate only subdivisions and do not imply contrariety. He is referred to Fichte's commentary.

7. Xavier Léon, in, *Fichte et son Temps*, II, pp. 101–104, makes a parallel with Babeuf.

8. G. W. F. Hegel, *Early Theological Writings*, tr. by W. M. Knox (Chicago, 1948), p. 312, from *Hegels theologische Jugendschriften* (Tübingen: von H. Nohl, 1907), p. 348.

9. The first two formulas are brought together in Jacques Taminiaux, *La Nostalgie de la Grèce à l'aube de l'idéalisme allemand* (La Haye, 1967), p. 234. Among recent interpreters, only Michael Theunissen and to a lesser extent Charles Taylor (see note 11 below) have, to my knowledge, acknowledged clearly the hierarchical aspect of those formulas. Theunissen mentions them repeatedly, indeed their common matrix is central to his general argument, in *Hegels Lehre vom absoluten Geist als theologisch-politischer Traktat* (Berlin: de Gruyter, 1970), pp. 8, 15–16, 35, 47–9, 50, 55–6, 68, 72, 126–7, 161–3, etc.

10. Even with Theunissen, the "encompassing of the contrary," if it surfaces here and there, is not systematically isolated, and perhaps for this reason early formulas are brought to bear indiscriminately on later texts where they may not always be relevant (as when Hegel is corrected, pp. 126–7, or about the infinite, pp. 8, 49).

11. Charles Taylor, *Hegel* (Cambridge: Cambridge University Press, 1975), pp. 240–44, esp. p. 242 *init.*

12. This movement seems to me somehow implied by Taylor, *Hegel*: first (p. 240), "the Hegelian notion of infinity is of a whole which is not conditioned or bounded by something

else," then (p. 242), "of a whole whose inner articulation and process unfolds of necessity," and finally (p. 244), of "the life inherent in the coming to be and passing away of the finite."

13. Theunissen, *Hegel Lehre.*

14. On Herder and on the conception of the nation, see *Dumont,* "Aspects."

15. Hegel, *Early Theological Writings (Hegels Theologische Jugendschriften), passim.* Most characteristic is the passage on pp. 265–66 (original) or p. 211 (English translation).

9. The Duty to Desire: Love, Friendship, and Sexuality in Some Puritan Theories of Marriage

Edmund Leites

When philosophers or political scientists look for early statements of some modern Western ideas of marriage, they are likely to turn to Locke's *Two Treatises of Government,* for there we find elements or hints of the modern view that marriage is a contractual relation between two autonomous and equal partners. Husband and wife jointly set the terms of their relationship; their particular interests determine its character; they retain the freedom to leave when the terms of the contract are no longer satisfied. In this search of forerunners, however, it is a mistake to limit one's reading of seventeenth-century texts to Locke's. In the following pages, I hope to persuade you that a number of seventeenth-century English theologians and preachers, for the most part Puritan, deserve equal attention. I shall consider William Ames and Richard Baxter, two of the most important casuists for seventeenth-century Puritans; Thomas Gataker, William Gouge, and Daniel Rogers, three Puritan clergymen who distinguished themselves particularly in their writings on marriage; and Jeremy Taylor, who was no Puritan, but whose attitudes toward marriage were in many respects like those of the Puritan casuists and theologians.

By calling someone "Puritan," I mean to say that he or she was part of the sixteenth- and seventeenth-century popular movement to reform English Christianity. In spite of the many divisions within this movement, there are general features which characterize all the intellectual and social tendencies I call "Puritan." Puritans demanded that they and others lead a life which was, in the realm of everyday conduct, ethically strict; in the realm of belief, meticulously scrupulous; in matters of ritual, simple (thus they were suspicious of cross and mitre, surplice and relic); and in matters of piety, deeply concerned with the inward state of the soul (thus they were hostile to a church satisfied with the perfunctory performance of outward acts).[1] This piety, as we shall see, has its analogue in the Puritans' notion of conjugal love: an outward fulfillment of the duties of marriage was not enough; the proper intentions and feelings toward your spouse must also exist.

A few reflections on the Roman Catholic background of Puritan ideas are in order. Let us begin with the Roman Catechism of 1566, "a careful distillation of Counter-reformation theology," in which we find a statement of the ends of marriage as established by God; we should seek at least one of them in marrying, although we may have other ends as well. It tells us that the first of the appropriate ends is the

> ... very partnership of diverse sexes—sought by natural instinct, and compacted in the hope of mutual help so that one aided by the other may more easily bear the discomforts of life and sustain the weakness of old age. Another is the appetite of procreation, not so much that heirs of property and riches be left, but that worshippers of the true faith and religion be educated ... And this is the one cause why God instituted marriage at the beginning. . . . The third is one which after the fall of the first parent was added to the other causes, . . . [for man's] appetite began to fight with right reason; so indeed he who is conscious of his weakness and does not wish to bear the battle of the flesh may use the remedy to avoid the sins of lust.[2]

In making companionship, specifically, mutual support and comfort, one of the chief purposes of marriage, indeed, in listing companionship first among these purposes, the authors of the catechism went against those within the Catholic world, such as Augustine, who made little of this side of marriage. Genesis (2. 18-23) tells us that God did not find it good for man to be alone; therefore, he gave Adam a helpmeet: woman, bone of his bone, flesh of his flesh; she pleased him greatly. But why, asks Augustine (*De Genesi ad Litteram Libri Duodecim*, 9. 7) did Adam need a *woman* to be his helpmeet? As far as he can see, he replies, she would have been of no use to him, or any man, if she had not been capable of bearing children: "Non itaque video, ad quod aliud adiutorium mulier facta sit viro, si generandi causa substrahitur." What, then, of woman as delightful companion to man, comforter, supporter? What of man as this to woman? This receives scant mention in the theology of Augustine, who was, in matters of marriage, sexuality, and the status of woman, often more liberal than other Fathers of the Church. In his commentary on Genesis (9. 7), he repeats what he had said some years before in *De Bono Coniugale*:

the goods of marriage are three, *fides, proles, sacramentum*. *Fides*, "fidelity," includes paying the marriage debt as well as keeping from intercourse with others; *proles*, the good of offspring, includes the support and education of children as well as their creation; marriage is a *sacramentum*, a "symbol of stability," therefore indissoluble. None of these goods, as Noonan convincingly argues, includes the delight in the companionship and comfort which a man and a woman can give to each other.[3]

Within the medieval and early modern Roman Church, Aristotle's *Nichomachean Ethics* sustained those who sought to give a more honored place to marriage as friendship. In the *Ethics*, Aristotle says that marriage is a kind of friendship, indeed, one more natural to human beings than the friendship of those who constitute the polis (*Nichomachean Ethics* 1162^{a}15–20). True, we are by nature political animals (*Politics* 1253^{a}5–10), but we are even more inclined to form couples than we are to form cities. We are, as it is put in the Latin Aristotle upon which Thomas commented, "in natura coniugale magis quam politicam" (Thomas Aquinas, *Sententia Libri Ethicorum* 8. 12).

Aristotle sees three grounds for friendship: friends can be useful to each other, they can delight in one another's company (for a variety of reasons), and they can love one another's virtue. All three are available to the married couple. Spouses can be useful to each other in the running of a household, they can please and delight each other in their sexual relations, and they can love one another's virtue, if they are virtuous (*Nichomachean Ethics* 1162^{a}25–30). Marriage love is special, for it can unite into one all the kinds of friendship we can ever have: virtuous men can love each other for their virtue; youths typically love each other for sheer pleasure; old men may well be friends because it is useful to them, since people "at that age pursue not the pleasant but the useful" (*Nichomachean Ethics* 1156^{a}5–1156^{b}10). Spouses, however, may love one another for all these reasons, at any stage of life.

The idea of marriage as friendship is taken up by Thomas.[4] Indeed, he relies upon Aristotle's notion that there must be a certain equality in all relationships to defend his belief that a man can have only one wife at a time. If reason deems it improper for a woman to have several husbands at one time, as it does, then, Thomas argues, it is wrong for a man to have several wives at one time, for marriage is a friendship, and "equality is a condition of friendship." "Were it lawful for a man to have several wives," but not lawful for a wife to have several husbands, "the friendship of a wife for her husband would not be freely bestowed, but servile as it were," for she would not be his true equal. "And this argument," says Thomas, "is confirmed by experience: since where men have several wives, the wives are treated as servants" (*Summa Contra Gentiles* 3. 124).

"The greatest friendship" seems to be between spouses, Thomas writes, for husband and wife "are made one not only in the act of carnal intercourse, which even among dumb animals causes an agreeable fellowship, but also as partners in the whole intercourse of daily life: so that, to indicate this, man must leave father and mother (Gen. 2. 24) for his wife's sake" (*Summa Contra Gentiles* 3. 123).

The approach of Aristotle and Thomas to marriage lives on in the sixteenth-century Roman catechism from which I quoted earlier. The same belief that marriage is a friendship, and a source of mutual delight and comfort, sustains some of the liberalizing tendencies within the late medieval and early modern church concerning sexual delight within marriage. Augustine took the position that God warrants and permits the pleasure and delight of intercourse among spouses only to the extent that it furthers the end of procreation: "What food is for the health of man, intercourse is for the health of the species, and each is not without carnal delight which cannot be lust, if modified and restrained by temperance, it is brought to a natural use," that is, done for the sake of procreation (*De Bono Coniugale* 16. 18). Unlike Aristotle, he did not think of sexual delight as a constituent of marriage friendship. Aristotle's belief remained alive in spite of Augustine. It was fully presented by Thomas in his commentary on the philosopher's *Ethics*; moreover, Thomas accepts Aristotle's outlook, although he does not make much of it, in the *Summa Contra Gentiles* (3. 123). The Scotsman John Major, professor of theology at the Universities of Paris, Glasgow, and St. Andrews during the first half of the sixteenth century, does much more with it. In his commentary on the sentences of Peter Lombard, he writes that "whatever men say, it is difficult to prove that a man sins in knowing his own wife for the sake of having pleasure," for husband and wife marry not only to have children, but to provide "consolation" to one another.[5] Others argued for the opinion permitting intercourse between spouses for pleasure on different grounds; the defense of this opinion in the seventeenth century provoked fierce opposition from rigorists within the Church, especially the theologians of Louvain, led by the Irishman John Sinnigh, who called the opinion permitting intercourse for pleasure "brutish."[6]

John Major did not go so far as to make the life of the married equal or superior in merit to the life of committed celibates. But the doctrine that celibacy is the superior state, vigorously defended by writers like Jerome and Chrysostom in the ancient world,[7] and upheld by Thomas (close as he was to Aristotle), was not to go unchallenged in the sixteenth century. What could be more honorable or holy than matrimony, Erasmus asks in his *Encomium Matrimonii*;[8] since its author was not Lycurgus, Moses, or Solon, but God himself:

For at the begynnyng when he had made man of the slyme of the
erthe he thought that his lyfe shoulde be utterly myserable and
unpleasaunt, if he joyned not Eve a compagnion unto him ... Now
syr if the other sacramentes of Christes chyrch be had in great
veneration, who seeth nat that moch worshyppe ought to be gyven
to this, which was both ordeyned of god, & fyrst of all other? And
the other in erth, this in paradise/the other for remedy/this for
solas/the other were put to in helpe of nature ... which was fallen,
only this was gyven to nature at the fyrst creation.[9]

"Bachelershyp," Erasmus tells a friend who is unwilling to marry, is "a
forme of lyvnge bothe barren and unnaturall," whereas nothing could be
more natural than wedlock, so much so that all peoples, no matter how
barbarous, deem it holy.[10] God has deeply imprinted the need and desire
for marriage love not only upon us, but upon other species, for "the sense
and feelynge" of marriage love "hath not only perced the turtyls/and the
doves/but also the most cruell wyld bestes. For the lyons be gentil and
meeke to theyr lyonnesses" (sig. B5ᵛ). Whosoever, therefore, "is not
touched with desyr of wedlocke seemeth no man, but a stone/an ennemy
to nature/a rebelle to God/by his owne foly sekynge hys decay and
undoynge" (sig. B4ᵛ–[B5ʳ]).

Christ said that those who gelded themselves for the kingdom of God
were blessed (Matt. 19), but the Lord's word appertained to those times
"when it was expedient to be most redy & lose from all worldy
bussynesses." Today, surely, Erasmus says, "the most holy kynd of lyfe is
wedlocke puerly & chastly kept" (sig. Ciᵛ). And in this bond, duty and
pleasure need not be enemies:

> ... if the most parte of thynges (yea whyche be also bytter) ar of a
> good man to be desyred for none other purpose, but bycause they
> be honeste, matrimony doutles is chefely to be desyred whereof a
> man may dout whether it hath more honesty than plesure [.] For
> what thynge is sweeter, then with her to lyve, with whome ye may
> be most streghtly copuled, not onely in the benevolence of the
> mynd, but also in the coniunction of the body (sig. [C6ʳ]).

The "plesure of bodyes is the leste parte of the goodes that wedlock
hathe" (sig. [C8ᵛ]), yet it is not to be despised. It has

> ... bene rightly every where pronounced as a proverbe, that *god nor
> nature have made no thynge frustrate nor in vayne*/why (I pray you)
> hath god geven us these members? why these pryckes and
> provocations? why hath he added the power of begettynge, if
> bachelarshyp be taken for a prayse? (sig. [B7ᵛ]).

The member is meant to be used. "If one wold gyve you a pretious gyfte, as a bowe/a garment/or a swerde, ye shuld seme unworthy [of] the thyng that ye have receyved, if outher ye wolde nat, or ye could nat use it" (sig. [B7ᵛ]). He who is not taken with the pleasures of earthly love—so sweetly coupled with fond devotion within marriage—"certes," says Erasmus (sig. [C8ᵛ]). "I would cal hym no man but a playne stone." Nothing can be said for the man content with bachelorhood. "What is more hatefull then the man which (as though he were borne only to hymselfe) lyveth for hymselfe, seketh for hymselfe/spareth for hymselfe/doth cost to hymselfe, loveth no persone, is loved of no persone?" (sig. [C8ʳ]).

Erasmus was not alone in his advocacy of the superiority of the married state over virginity; Wives took the same position, and Todd[11] argues that a substantial number of sixteenth-century Catholics and Anglicans did the same. Yet the fate of the ideas of Erasmus and his like was not altogether a happy one. On the continent, the Council of Trent declared the view that marriage is superior to celibacy "anathema."[12] In 1547, the Sorbonne put the *Encomium Matrimonii* on the index of prohibited books.[13] In the "large" catechism of Cardinal Bellarmine, the *Dichiarazione piu copiosa della dottrina cristiana* (1598), of great influence in the seventeenth-century Church, the "Student" asks, "Whether it is better to take the Sacrament of Matrimonie or to kepe virginitie?" The "Master" replies,

> The Apostel S. Paul hath cleared this doubt, having written that he who joyneth himself in Mariage doth wel, but he that doth not joyne himself, but kepeth virginite doth better. And the reason is, because Mariage is a thing humane, Virginitie is Angelical. Mariage is according to nature, Virginitie is above nature. And not only virginitie but widowhood is also better than mariage. Therefore whereas our Saviour said in a parable, that the good sede yelded in one fild thirtie fold fruite, in an other threescore, in an other a hundred fold: the holie Doctors have declared, that the thirtie fold fruite is of Matrimonie, the threescore fold of widowhood, the hundreth fold of virginitie.[14]

In England, whose humanists had perhaps taught Erasmus something about marriage,[15] the union of erotic, spiritual, domestic, and ethical bonds in one marriage ideal, the notion of marriage as the best sort of friendship, and the idea that it is the best sort of life for man and woman, fared rather better a success which no doubt owed something to the Church of England's rejection of institutionalized celibacy, in both monastic orders and the life of the secular priest. From the second half of the sixteenth century, students at Oxford and Cambridge "encountered a university curriculum that included the words of . . . Erasmus, Jean Luis Vives and Thomas More." Preachers cited them, and the scholarly and pious made their works part of their collections.[16] And from the 1620s to the 1660s, a flood of often superbly written texts on marriage came forth, largely from Puritan pens. "Let al Papists, Jesuites, Priests, or others," writes Rogers,[17] "with all their fomenters and adherents, tremble and be ashamed, who have dared so many times dishonour marriage, and so many wayes to defile it." "They know not the benefit of the married estate," writes Gouge, "who prefer single life before it." He calls upon "the admirerers and praisers of a single estate" to "bring forth all their reasons, and put them in the other scole against marriage. If these two be duly poised, and rightly weyed," he says, "we should find single life too light to be compared with honest marriage."[18]

What is so good about married life? Gouge offering a trinity of reasons already well-established within the Catholic and Angelican world, says it is for procreation, the avoidance of fornication, and mutual aid: "No such helpe," writes Gouge, "can man have from any other creature as from a wife; or a woman, as from an husband."[19]

Like Erasmus, Puritans argue for the excellence of marriage by pointing out that it was instituted by God *before* humankind had fallen; it was not simply a remedy for our concupiscence (though that it became, once we fell). It was part of the paradisical state itself. But why did Adam need a wife? Why did he need to better his condition in this way? What was wrong with Paradise without Eve? The Puritans do not share the outlook of Augustine, who thought that she would have been of no use to Adam had she not been the bearer of his children. For the Puritans, she was also his *companion*: it was not good that he was *alone* (Gen. 2. 18), and he needed a woman for a companion, as she needed a man. Secker puts it well:

> When all other creatures had their mates, *Adam* wanted his: Though he was the Emperor of the Earth, and the Admiral of the Seas, yet in Paradise without a companion, though he was truly happy yet he was not fully happy; Though he had enough for his board, yet he had not enough for his bed; Though he had many creatures to serve him, yet he wanted a creature to solace him; when he was compounded in creation, he must be compleated by conjunction; when he had no sinne to hurt him, then he must have a wife to help him; *It is not good that man should be alone.*[20]

Therefore, God determined to make him a helpmeet. But as Gouge writes, none of the birds or beasts that God had already created would do, so Adam's creator created woman out of "mans substance and side, and after his image." Her maker then presented Eve to Adam for his consideration. The first man manifested "a good liking to her," so God gave her to him "to bee his wife." Thus "the inviolable law of the neer and firm union of man and wife" was first "enacted."[21]

It is true, before Adam had Eve, he had God, but this was not enough to remove his loneliness; nor could it be assuaged by the creatures that already "lived on the earth, or breathed the air." He needed a woman; and once a woman was created, she needed a man.

The cure of Adam's loneliness was to be love: his love for Eve, and her love for him; Eve's loneliness would be cured in the same way. Marriage provides this balm. The Puritans say that men must love their wives, and wives, their husbands; this is a duty that flows out of one of the purposes for which marriage was first instituted: thus Gouge tells us that there must be "mutuall love betwixt man and wife ... else the end and right use of marriage will be perverted." Baxter tells us in firm tones that *"the first Duty of Husbands is to Love their Wives (and Wives their Husbands) with a true intire Conjugal Love."* "Conjugal Love" is a "mayne and joint duty of the married," says Rogers.[22]

The Puritans' appreciation of conjugal love was accompanied by an acute awareness of how bad a bad marriage was; their sense of this was no doubt sharpened by their appreciation of the pleasures and comfort of a happily married life. Marriage, writes Gataker "is *a business* of the *greatest consequence,* and that whereon the maine comfort or discomfort of a mans life doth depend; that which may make *thine house* to bee as *an heaven* or *an hell* here upon earth."[23]

"They that enter into the state of marriage," writes Jeremy Taylor,[24] who is in accord with the Puritans on this matter, "cast a dye of the greatest contingency, and yet of the greatest interest in the world, next to the last throw for eternity." A happy marriage provides a joy that lasts throughout life, an unhappy one creates lasting sorrow for both spouses. A wife "hath no sanctuary to retire to, from an evill husband; she must remain at home, the very source of her unhappiness, to "dwell upon her sorrow." A husband can run "from many hours of his sadness, yet he must return to it again, and when he sits among his neighbours he remembers the objection that lies in his bosome, and he sighs deeply." Puritan authors sometimes referred to the words of Augustine, who, on more than one occasion, said that a bad marriage is like a bad conscience: you cannot get away from it. When love is absent between husband and wife, writes Baxter, it is like "a Bone out of joynt; there is no *ease,* no *order"* between them, till they are set right again.[25]

II

The love required in marriage is more than a general good will or benevolence towards one's spouse; it is more than the Christian charity we may bear toward many: instead, it is a special sort of love which is required only of the married.[26] For one thing, as Erasmus had indicated, it is sensual, as well as spiritual. Rogers tells us that "by conjugall love," he means "not only Christian love, a grace of God's spirit: (for marriage borders much what upon nature and flesh) nor yet a carnall and sudden flash of affection, completely enflamed by concupiscense: (rather brutish than humane) but a sweet compounde of both, religion and nature." which is "properly called *Marriage* love."[27]

Marriage was instituted to provide mutual support and comfort; sensuous delight in the body of one's spouse is an essential element of the comfort which marriage must provide: thus to take (and encourage) delight is a duty which falls equally on both spouses: "Husband and wife," writes Baxter, "*must take delight in Love, and company, and converse of each other.*" Gataker tells us that one of a husband's duties of "love" toward his wife is "*Joy & delight in her.*"[28] He continues with a passage from *Proverbs*, often quoted by Puritan writers on marriage: "*Drinke*, saith the wise man [of *Proverbs*], *the water of thine own cisterne*: . . . *and rejoyce in the wife of thy youth: Let her be with thee as a loving Hind, and the pleasant Roe*: Let her brests or bosome *content thee at all times: and delight continually*, or as the word there is, even *doate on the Love of her*" (Proverbs 5: 15, 18, 19).[29]

This sensuous love is not simply permitted, given the existence of a higher, holier, 'spritual' relation between man and wife, nor is it allowed only to forward the other purposes of marriage. It is required as a constituent and intrinsic element of a good marriage. This sensual affection and delight must continue unabated, with the full intensity of youthful desire, throughout the whole of married life. "*Keep up your Conjugal Love in a constant heat and vigor*," writes Baxter.[30] From the very onset, your spouse must be the apple of your eye. As life goes on, you must delight in your spouse as if he or she were your new and youthful husband or bride: Gataker writes that you must not suffer your "*love to grow luke-warme.*"[31]

Physical deformities may not weaken your enjoyment of your spouse. If there are (objectively) more beautiful women or handsome men, disadvantageous comparisons should not be made: the pleasure you take in your spouse should be so great, there should be no place for any defect.[32] Counseling the wife, Rogers says, "Poare upon your own husband, and his parts, let him be the vaile of your eies, as *Abimelec* told *Sara*, and looke no further." Then counseling the husband, he says, let your wife "bee your furthest object: thinke you no virtues in any beyonde hers: those that are but small, yet make them great by oft contemplation: those that are greater, esteeme and value at their due rate." Gouge (1626: 208) writes that "an husband's *affection* to his wife must be answerable to his *opinion* of her: hee ought therefore *to delight in his wife intirely, that is, so to delight in her, as wholly and only delighting in her* . . . if a man have wife, not very beautiful, or proper, but having some deformity in her body," he should nonetheless "delight in her, as if she were the finest and every way most compleat woman in the world."[33]

The whole character of the love required, then, is this: spouses should find their mates to be the most special and delightful persons in their lives, throughout their lives. The Puritans who uphold this view are far from being hostile to romance; indeed, they make romance a duty of married life.[34]

Marriage is by no means only a sensual relation for the Puritan theorists of marriage; spouses must also be spiritually devoted to each other. Baxter tells us that "*A principal duty between husband and wife, is, with special care, and skill, and diligence, to help each other in the knowledge, and obedience of God, in order to their salvation.*"[35] This, too, is an obligation which falls upon both husband and wife: wives as well as husbands may criticize their spouses; thoughts, feelings, and actions out of a concern for their spiritual and moral well-being. Wives who are normally required to be docile and submissive thus have a certain freedom to be openly critical of their husbands—in the service (or apparent service) of God, of course.

Baxter urged husbands and wives to pray together "in private," as well as with the larger family, which includes children and servants. Gouge made conjugal prayer one of the duties of marriage. He tells us that the need for "a true, spiritual, matrimonial love" between husband and wife is one of the things "most meet to be mentioned in private prayer betwixt" them; spouses should pray "that such needful gifts and graces as are wanting in either of them may be wrought: and such vices and infirmities as they are subject unto may be rendered."[36]

Such prayer between husband and wife provided one private occasion where wives could openly criticize their husbands. We need not simply *assume* that they did so: Baxter tells us, with startling frankness, that his late wife

> . . . was very desirous that we should all have lived in a constancy of Devotion, and a blameless Innocency: And in this respect she was the meetest helper that I could have had in the world (the ever I was

acquainted with): For I was apt to be over-careless in my Speech, and too backward in my Duty; And [at her death] she was still endavoring to bring me to greater wariness and strictness in both: If I spake rashly or sharply, it offended her: If I carried it (as I was apt) with too much neglect of Ceremony, or humble Complement to any, she would modestly tell me of it: If my very Looks seemed not pleasant, she would have me amend them (which my weak pained state of Body undisposed me to do:) If I forgat any Week to Catechize my Servants, and familiarly instruct them (besides my ordinary Family-Duties) she was troubled at my remisness. And whereas of late years my decay of Spirits, and deseased heaviness and pain, made me much more seldom and cold in profitable Conference and Discourse in my house, then I had been when I was younger, and had more Ease, and Spirits, and natural Vigour, she much blamed me, and was troubled at it, as a wrong to her self and others: ... [though] of late years, my constant weakness and pain ... [kept me much in] my bed, that I was seldomer in secret Prayer with my Wife then she desired.[37]

This freedom of wives to criticise their husbands creates a tension within the Puritan conception of marriage: for the Puritans are firmly convinced that men must rule and wives must obey. Gataker approvingly quotes Colossians (3. 18): *"Wives, submit yourselves unto your Husbands, as it is comely in the Lord."*[38] When thinking along these lines, the Puritans call for restraint in feeling as well as submission in action. Women must restrain their expressions of anger and discontent, even if their husbands' conduct gives them good grounds. Docility and a loving gentleness toward husbands are prime wifely virtues. This wifely restraint was to be balanced, according to the theorists of marriage, by husbands' gentle and restrained use of their own authority.[39]

Life is not all authority and submission; the Puritans knew that they lived in a material world of food and drink, bedstead and fireplace. Thus they said that husband and wife must also care for each other's material and worldly comfort. Men who do not care for the physical well-being of their wifes are severely condemned; prudence in managing household affairs is one of the chief virtues of a wife.[40] Gataker tell us that

It is no shame or staine ... for a woman to be housewifely, be she never so well borne, be she never so wealthy. For it is the *womans trade* so to be: it is the end of her *creation*; it is that she was made for. She was made for man, and given to man, not to be a *playfellow*, or a *bed-fellow*, or a *table-mate*, onely with him, (and yet to be all these too,) but to be a *yoake-fellow*, a *worke-fellow*, a *fellow labourer* with him, to be *an assistant* and *an helper* unto him, in the managing of such *domesticall and household affaires*.[41]

Thus the prospect that a woman is prudent ought to weigh heavily when a man is choosing a mate. The wives of not a few eminent ministers in both Old and New England handled all the financial affairs of the family, leaving their husbands with greater liberty to concern themselves with matters spiritual and ecclesiastical; the men praised their women for this in no uncertain terms.[42]

Some writers put this obligation to care for the ethical, religious, and worldly well-being of one's spouse in the words that will remind you of Aristotle and Thomas: they say that husband and wife must be *the best of friends*; you may have no greater friend than your spouse. It may be asked, says Taylor, "whether a friend may be more than Husband or Wife" to you? To which he answers,

> . . . it can neither be reasonable or just, prudent or lawful: but the reason is, because marriage is the Queen of friendships, in which there is a communication of all that can be communicated by friendship . . . other friendships are a part of this [marriage friendship], they are marriages too, less indeed then the other, because they cannot, must not, be all the indearment which they other is; yet that being the principal, is the measure of the rest, and all to be honoured by like dignities, and measured by the same rules, . . . friendships are *Marriages* of the soul, and of fortunes and interests, and counsels . . . [as] they are brotherhoods too . . . [13]

The Puritans were familiar with Cicero's *De Amicitia* as well as Aristotle's *Ethics*, but they are closer to Aristotle than they are to Cicero, for the Roman thinks that friendship can occur only among *men*. Cicero finds much of the meaning of friendship in politics and war, although he thinks it can be enjoyed by those who have honorably retired from these worlds. By their own example, friends must encourage each other to act honorably in these harsh realms: we can love virtuous men "whom we have never seen," says Cicero (*De Amicitia* 8. 28–29); "now," he continues, "if the force of integrity is so great that we love it . . . in those we have never seen, . . . what wonder that men's souls are stirred when they think they see clearly the virtue and goodness of those with whom a close intimacy is possible?" Cicero offers Gaius Luscinus Fabricius, the Roman general and consul of the early third century B.C., notable, to later Romans, as a model of the integrity and simplicity which marked the mores of earlier days, as an example of a man whom he and his contemporaries have never seen, but love. As the tale is told, Fabricius resisted attempts to bribe him; thus, in spite of his high offices, he died poor; provision had to be made for his daughter out of funds of the state.

Women such as Fabricius' daughter could suffer or enjoy a fate created by the virtue of fathers and husbands in politics and war, but they were not, for Cicero, ordinarily active participants in these realms. They were not the stuff out of which friends could be made. Cicero held to the notion that women were by nature weak and light-minded (*infirmitas sexus* and *levitas animi*), although his experience of his first wife, Terentia, should have made him doubt this belief. In his own time, some aristocratic women did take an active part in Roman political life, but none of them were models of political virtue for Cicero; he retained his admiration for the manners and morals of the early Romans, who, with some exceptions, reserved the worlds of politics and war to men.

Eros, too, prevents wives and husbands from being true friends. Although friendship meant devotion, for Cicero, and a delight in being together, it is not an erotic relation, nor one in which *eros* is welcome. He disapproves of the homosexual friendships of Greek culture to which some Romans of his own time were drawn. Homosexual intercourse is unnatural, says Cicero (*Tusculan Disputations*). The poet Ennius writes that "shame's beginning is the stripping of men's bodies openly"; Cicero agrees: the shameful practice of homosexual friendship had its origin, he thinks, "in the Greek gymnasia" (*Tusculans* 4. 70).

In general, he suspects sexuality, including the love of a man for a woman, "to which nature has granted wider tolerance" than it has to male homosexuality (*Tusculans* 4. 71). In sexual pleasure and sexual longing, we lose the temperate, peaceful, and equable mood which the wise man seeks to have at all times (*Tusculans* 4. 30ff). He condemns Aristotle and the Peripatetics, who say that there is a proper place in our life for the agitated movement of our soul if they are not excessive. This view, he says, "must be regarded as weak and effeminate," *mollis et enervata*. "Those who are transported with delight at the enjoyment of sexual pleasures are degraded," he writes; "those who covet them with feverish soul are criminal. . . . In fact, the whole passion ordinarily termed love [*amor*] . . . is of such exceeding triviality that I see nothing that I think comparable with it" (*Tusculans* 4. 38–39, 68). It is worse than trivial, for it leads us to do foolish and dishonorable things.

In their conception of marriage love, the Puritans reject Cicero's attitude toward women, friendship, and sexuality. Husband and wife are to be the best of friends; sensuality and sexuality are to be integral parts of this friendship: friendship and erotic romance go hand in hand. The unselfish devotion that men were to have for each other in the Ciceronian tradition must give way, not to a new world of unqualified egoism toward all, but to a kind of friendship with one's wife that was never called for by the Roman senator.

In this notion of marriage love, many of the themes of classical and medieval texts on friendship, including some of Cicero's, are retained or given different form. The Puritans do not think that a major element of the friendship between husband and wife is the mutual encouragement to honorable action in politics and war, yet they do conceive of marriage friendship as one which should ethically and spiritually nourish husband and wife, whatever their callings. Then again, while Cicero does not make the usefulness of friends in practical matters the fundamental principle of friendship, he does give it a place: your true friends will help you in politics and business if they can. The Puritans, too, see husband and wife as joined in practical affairs, though not matters of state; let the reader recall Gataker's comment that woman was made to be a "*yoake-fellow*" as well as a "*play-fellow*" to man, a "fellow *labourer* . . . in the managing of . . . *domesticall and household affairs*."

Some notions are lost. Cicero thought friends must nourish each other in the realm of letters, manners, conversation, and thought, in short, in the realm of urbane culture.[44] The Puritans did not think that marriage had this purpose, nor, for that matter, did Cicero, which may be one more reason why he did not think of marriage as a kind of friendship. There are some starling new notions, as well, in the Puritan idea of marriage friendship. The same Puritans who believed that husband and wife should concern themselves with the ethical and spiritual character of their spouse also believed that one of the greatest goods of life is *being loved* by one's spouse. This love is a great good not because it leads our husband or wife to lavish great gifts on us, or do whatever we say, but because the love itself is comforting: someone cares for us, delights in us; we are no longer alone in the world. In the works of Aristotle, Cicero, and in the New Testament, this is a theme that is hardly to be found, if at all: it is a great good to *be loved* by another human; above all, it is a great good for a man, if he is loved by a woman, and a great good for a woman, if she is loved by a man. This idea is a foundation of the Puritan theory of marriage.

Much of this idea is found in Jeremy Taylor's thought. Objecting to the exalted belief that we should love a friend only for his virtue and not for what we hope from him, Taylor (1662: 29–31) writes, "although I love my friend because he is worthy, yet he is not worthy if he can do no good." But what kind of good? True, "he is onely fit to be chosen for a friend who can give me counsel, or defend my cause, or guide me right, or relieve me, or can and will, when I need it, do me good: onely this I adde: into the heapes of doing good, I will reckon" *loving me*, "for it is a pleasure to be beloved." Marriage is the model of all other human friendships, for in no other relation with a man or woman, can we be loved so well.[45]

In a full-scale attempt to see Puritan ideas of marriage as part of the history of friendship, both in idea and practice, we should not ignore Montaigne, who shares much with Cicero. As far as friendship goes, *none* of "the four ancient forms of association—natural, social, hospitable, erotic," writes Montaigne, "come up to real friendship, either separately, or together." The love of women "is more active, more scorching, and more intense" than that of true friendship. "But it is an impetuous and fickle flame, undulating and variable a fever flame, subject to fits and lulls, that holds only by one corner. In friendship it is a general and universal warmth, moderate and even, besides a constant and settled warmth, all gentleness and smoothness, with nothing bitter and stinging about it."[46]

Montaigne thinks that the logics of desire in friendship and in our love of women are quite different. Adopting the view so characteristic of the Roman poet Martial, Montaigne thinks that a man's full possession of a woman destroys his desire for her: "la jouyssance le perd"; we become satiated, uninterested.[47] Friendship is different; the more it is enjoyed, the more it is desired. The pleasure of a woman's friendship must thus deprive a man of his desire for her: to the extent that he desires her, she must not be his, but what is the pleasure of her friendship without his secure knowledge of her love for him?

But what of marriage, which is supposed to be a stable relation? A man cannot even hope that he and his wife will be friends, for friendship must be freely given, but marriage "is a bargain to which only the entrance is free—its continuance being constrained and forced, depending otherwise than on our will—and a bargain ordinarily made for other ends." Montaigne who devotes a remarkable essay to the memory of his friend, They commonly lack the "capacity" (perhaps he means the powers of spirit and mind) which sustain the "communion and fellowship" of friendship; "nor does their soul seem firm enough to endure the strain of so tight and durable a knot."[48] Who can be surprised that the same Montaigne who devotes aremarkable essay to the memory of his friend, Etienne de la Boétie, makes but little and passing mention of his wife? The distance between Montaigne and Puritans is great: I need only mention the extraordinary records of conjugal devotion left by Richard Baxter (1681), in his memoir of his wife, and by Lucy Hutchinson, in her memoir of her husband, written for the sake of her children.[49]

III

Benjamin Nelson, in his extraordinary essay on the history of friendship in the West, says that the older ideal of an unselfish devotion of a man to his friend gave way, in early modern Europe, to a new view, unsympathetic to this devotion. He believes this shift in attitude is part of a larger passage in the West from the older world views of "tribal brotherhood" to the newer one of "universal otherhood" *not* universal brotherhood. The older idea of friendship, in which devotion was but to one or a few, did not become a basis for a new and triumphal view in which devotion was to be given to every wider human groups; it was not successfully universalised. Instead, the idea of friendship came under attack and was ultimately replaced by an ethic which emphasised the disciplined pursuit of one's own personal good.[50]

The belief that a man should stand surety for a friend in need, even if this means the risk of all his wealth, is often part of medieval and Renaissance ideas of friendship. We find it dramatically and profoundly developed in Shakespeare's *Merchant of Venice*. Nelson describes sixteenth-century attacks on this expression of unlimited devotion to one's friend, the most striking of which is Luther's: "Standing surety is a work that is too lofty for a man; it is unseemly, for it is presumptuous and an invasion of God's rights. For . . . the scriptures bid us to put our trust and place our reliance on no man, but only on God; for human nature is false, vain, deceitful, and unreliable.[51] In this matter, Luther finds an ally in Sir Walter Raleigh, who tells his son,

> . . . suffer not thyself to be wounded for other men's faults, and scourged for other men's offences, which is the surety of another; for thereby millions of men have been beggared and destroyed, paying the reckoning of other men's riot, and the charge of other men's folly and prodigality; if thou smart, smart for thine own sins; and, above all things, be not made to carry the burdens of other men: if any friend desire thee to be his surety, give him a part of what thou hast to spare; if he press thee futher, he is not thy friend at all . . . [52]

No doubt, Nelson is right to say that in early modern Europe, the belief that friends ought to be devoted to one another without limit gave way, in *the realm of commerce*, to the belief that we ought to be governed by principles of rational business practice at all times, and make no exceptions on grounds of love or affection. The harshness of the world of commerce is not qualified by the idea that man should be a friend to man. The claims of friendship do not disappear from the world, however; indeed, in the sphere of marriage, they become more powerful than they ever were. In economic life, tribal brotherhood gives way to univeral otherhood, but in the realm of marriage, the belief in brotherhood and friendship moves forward. It is sad that the aristocratic idea of friendship among males could not become a norm governing *all* human relations, among *all* human beings, in all spheres of life. It did not simply give way, however, to another ethic in which friendship had no place; it would be better to say that the idea of friendship among males gave way to the love between husband and wife. The claims of friendship remained circumscribed in their application, "tribal," but they made their home, and they *still* make their home, in one of the most common relations of modern life. The world of commerce lost some of the restraints that might have mitigated its harshness, but the world of marriage gained an ethic, which if heeded at all, makes it more humane.

In a later essay, Nelson takes account of some of these developments: "too few seem to perceive that in the medieval world and in the early modern world—prior, actually, to the Puritans—a full religious sacralization of the family or family property did not exist. There did, indeed, not occur the sacralization of what might be called the special friendship with one's own wife."[53] He interprets the Puritan call for friendship with one's spouse, however, in a curious way: it is "the sacralization of a collective egoism of the family and its property." It is thus far from the ideal of male friendship in antiquity and the middle ages, which Nelson says "was conceived as the union that transcended all calculation and egotism whether of family or of person. From at least the time of Plato forward, the moralists and novelists insisted on preeminence of friendship, going so far as to deny that one's wife or member of one's family could truly be friends in the highest sense."

This is a prejudiced reading of friendship's twists and turns in history. Puritan marriage love is no more a collective egoism than the friendship among virtuous men espoused by Cicero. Cicero does call for a collective egoism among friends, for friends ought to favor each other over others. At the same time, this alliance has its limits: friends must not ask each other to do what is shameful; as we know, they must be exemplars of virtue to one another (*De Amicitia* 26, 35–40). The union of man and wife in Puritan thought is no less ethical.

IV

In the foregoing, I have described features of some seventeenth-century theories of marriage which bear significantly upon our understanding of contemporary American attitudes toward the union of man and wife. If we look to Locke's *Treatises of Government*, however, we will not find the complex of ideas just described. Locke, like Puritan and other seventeenth-century writers on marriage, believed that an agreement to marry had the character of a contract.[54] He was unlike them in thinking that spouses themselves should, in principle, have a great deal of latitude in setting the terms of this contract. Their freedom is not unlimited, for marriage does have natural purposes; spouses may not set terms which would impede their achievement. Marriage's chief purpose is "the continuation of the Species." This purpose, writes Locke, is not fulfilled simply by "procreation," it requires that "young Ones" be nourished and supported "till they are able to shift and provide for themselves." "Inheritance," too, must be "taken care for."[55] A man and a woman who have taken on this purpose by marrying must therefore remain together until all this is accomplished.

Locke also says that parental care and support is a "Right" of children; once created, a child has a rightful claim to aid "from his Parents" (78, 80). "Inheritance," too, is a "Natural" right of children (91–93), so their rights extend even beyond their youth; they have a claim against their parents as adults. These rights of children also mean that husband and wife must stay together. But for how long? When children can stand on their own two feet, when, moreover, their inheritance is taken care of, Locke sees no inherent reason why the marriage compact "may not be made determinable," that is, of limited duration, to end "either by consent, or at a certain time, or upon certain Conditions." This would make it like other "voluntary Compacts," which need not be made for life. There is no necessity in the nature of marriage, "nor to the ends of it, that it should always be for Life."[56] Indeed, beyond the natural purposes of marriage which bind the partners to certain terms, the ends of marriage should be set by the partners themselves: the terms of a marriage contract should answer the particular interests of those who wed.

Laslett notes that Locke was prepared to go even further than this. In his Journal, Locke made notes for the rules of a society based on reason alone, which he named "Atlantis." In this society, "he that is already married may marry another woman with his left hand . . . the ties, duration of conditions of the left hand marriage shall be no other than what is expressed in the contract of marriage between the parties."[57] (Perhaps he thinks that since the business of procreation is taken care of by the husband's first marriage, the parties to the second, "left hand" marriage are free to design their marriage as they wish.)

The difference between Locke's attitude and that of the Puritans can be readily seen if we compare the implicit theory of divorce and remarriage in Locke's *Second Treastise* with the explicit theory in Milton's tracts on divorce. From the point of view of pure reason, Locke thinks, mutual willingness to part is, within limits, sufficient to justify a complete divorce: a divorce which permits both parties to remarry. The reasons why they wish to part are not relevant; their wish to do so is enough. Parental obligations alone limit this freedom.

No Puritan writer shared this attitude; all strictly limited the grounds of divorce.[58] Most restricted these grounds to adultery and desertion; some argued that these grounds do not even permit a complete divorce, but only a separation; even the innocent party does not have the right to remarry. Milton was far bolder. Like many of his Puritan colleagues, he believes that the fundamental purpose of marriage is mutual support and comfort.[59] He therefore concludes that if differences in temperament between spouses make the fulfillment of this purpose impossible, divorce ought to be permitted, offering the opportunity to remarriage to both parties, although he leaves it up to the husband alone to decide whether a divorce shall occur. To yoke together a man and a woman who cannot give each other the warmth and comfort that marriage should give condemns them to a miserable life; to force them to maintain such a union defeats the purpose of marriage itself. Milton's argument that spouses may divorce when they are tempermentally incompatible reveals an attitude strikingly different from Locke's; for Milton argues his case in the light of the specific purposes of marriage. Spouses are not at liberty to aim at whatever ends they wish, but must guide themselves by the purposes of marriage as they are revealed by scripture and natural reason.

Locke and the Puritan theorists of marriage differ in other ways as well. Locke says that husbands should have the final say in marital disputes over things held in common, for the final decision having to be made by someone, "it naturally falls to the Man's share, as the abler and the stronger."[60] This subjection, however, is not basic to Locke's notion of marriage. We would not be far from his own viewpoint if we argued that husband and wife are equal and autonomous partners in marriage. In arguing for this, however, we would be far from the attitude of the Puritans, who make much of the submission of women to their husbands. We may therefore favor Locke; to be fair, let us keep in mind his failure to develop any conception of the emotional side of marriage as the Puritans do.

Clearly, there are Lockean currents in modern American conceptions of marriage: that husband and wife should meet each other as equals is one; that the interests and inclinations of husband and wife should be decisive in determining the character and objects of marriage is another. But in other respects, we might do better to look to the Puritan writers to find a source of some of our ideas of marriage. Four of their beliefs stand out in this respect: (1) that a chief end, or *the* chief end, of marriage is mutual support and comfort; (2) that sexual and sensual delight is essential to that comfort; (3) that husband and wife must also be the best of friends; (4) that this delight and friendship must last; neither may wane with the years.

V

In view of these ideas, how are we to evaluate Max Weber's belief that the "decisive characteristic" of the Puritans was their "asceticism" which "turned with all its force against one thing: the spontaneous enjoyment of life and all it had to offer"?[61] Much depends on a precise understanding of what Weber thinks asceticism is: a systematic self-discipline in feeling, intention, and action; which, if successful, means "the destruction of spontaneous, impulsive enjoyment." In the creation of such a discipline, writes Weber, lies "the great historical significance of Western monasticism." It

> ... developed a systematic method of rational conduct with the purpose of overcoming the *status naturae*, to free man from the power of irrational impulses and his dependence on the world and on nature. It attempted to subject man to the supremacy of a purposeful will, to bring his actions under constant self-control with a careful consideration of their ethical consequences . . . this active self-control . . . was also the most important practical ideal of Puritanism . . . like every rational type of asceticism, [it] tried to enable a man to maintain and act upon his constant motives, especially those which it taught him itself, against the emotions. In this formal psychological sense of the term, it tried to make him into a personality. Contrary to many popular ideas, the end of this asceticism was to be able to lead an alert, intelligent life: the most urgent task the destruction of spontaneous, impulsive enjoyment. The most important means [by which this asceticism achieved its end] was by bringing order into the conduct of its adherents.[62]

Weber is certainly correct in saying that the Puritan tried to make man "a personality," that is, sought to make him a being who acts "upon his constant motives" in all spheres of life, at all times. But the logic of self-control in the Puritan psychology of daily life is varied; it does not always involve hostility to spontaneous impulse in the name of psychic "order" and "methodical control," as Weber thinks.[63] In the case of married life, the Puritans called for an *integration* of ethics and impulse, constancy and spontaneity. The life of duty is a life of discipline, yet they make the spontaneous (and erotic) delight in one's spouse a *duty* of married life. Mutual delight in one another is not simply desirable, it is required: husband and wife together must make this a reality.[64]

Some might consider this odd, for how can one make such love a *duty*? Can romantic love truly be governed with the same rigor as the more emotionally neutral benevolence of eighteenth-century humanitarianism?

In *A Midsummer Night's Dream*, Hermia loves Lysander, as he loves her; Helena loves Demetrius, who loves not her, but Hermia. Yet once touched with the juice of Oberon's magic herb, Lysander has eyes only for Helena; a sign, he thinks, of his good judgment, for he says to his new-found love that "The will of man is by his reason sway'd;/And reason says you are the worthier maid" (*Midsummer Night's Dream* 2.2. 115–116). With further application of the juice of the same herb, Demetrius comes to love Helena Oberon's Titania even comes to love Bottom, with his ass's head. Titania tells Bottom she loves him, but Bottom replies, "Methinks, mistress, you should have little reason for that. And yet, to say the truth, reason and love have little company together now-a-days" (3. 1. 142–144). The happy resolution of the romantic tangles of *A Midsummer Night's Dream* are not solved by reason giving love its orders: we must have eyes for one another to love, but his is no work of reason: Oberon claims back Titania's love by another touch of her eyes. It is sweet magic, not cool logic, that does the trick.

From the point of view of Kant, and many contemporary moral philosophers, "ought" implies "can." Thus, love is beyond the rule of morals if it is wholly, and naturally, outside of our control. If it is so, then a fusion of ethics and eros in marriage love is beyond our control as well. This is Weber's conviction; like many German intellectuals and artists of the twentieth century, he thinks that rational self-discipline is no friend of erotic spontaneity: they are in harmony only in exceptional circumstances.[65] "Rarely," writes Weber, does life grant us the fusion of the two "in pure form." "He to whom it is given may speak of fate's fortune and grace—not of his own merit."[66]

The Puritans understood that there was something beyond reason's control in the love which must be found in marriage. It is mysterious, mysterious, writes Rogers, as the

> ... league of friendship, wherein we see God doth so order it, that by a secret instinct of love and sympathy, causing the heart of one to incline to the other, two friends have beene as one spirit in two bodies, as not only we see in *Jonathan* and *David*, but in heathens which have striven to lay downe their lives for the safeguard of each other ... oftimes a reason cannot be given by either partie, why they should be so tender each to other: it being caused not by any profitable or pleasurable means, but by mere sympathy, which is farre the more and noble cement of union, than what else so ever.[67]

There is a similar mystery at the heart of marriage love. Its causes are largely hidden and unknown; hence beyond our control: "the elme and the vine doe naturally so entwine and embrace each other, that its called, the friendly elme; who can tell why? much more then in reasonable creatures, it must be so."[68] Rogers even celebrates marriage love's distance from the dictates of cool judgement: "through this instrument of sympathie ... two consent together to become husband and wife," setting all others aside, although they are "more amiable in themselves, more rich, better bred, and the like." It must not be our own doing, but God's.

Others did not go this far, but agreed that love is rooted in temperamental affinities which we cannot rule.[69] If we are wrongly joined, happiness is beyond our reach. Yet an inability to love did not relieve a badly-yoked husband and wife from their duty to love one another; for the Puritans did not believe that "ought" implies "can" in matters of feeling, mood, temperament, motivation, and character, they saw us as under obligations we might not be able to fulfill without the aid of God's grace, which none of us can command.[70] Puritan casuists therefore counselled their readers to make a very careful choice of partner. It is not necessary to be deeply in love to marry, but a real likelihood that such love will develop is necessary. No one ought to marry a person he thinks he cannot, or is not likely, to love. This sense of one's affinity to a proposed spouse is of greater importance than the wishes of one's own parents, weighty as that is.[71]

Temperament is basic, but it is not all: Spouses can cultivate their delight in each other. The Puritans saw this cultivation as daily responsibility of spouses: "Put case," writes Rogers, that "thou hadst grounds of first love to thy companion: what then? thinkst thou that this edge will holde without dayly whetting?" To help couples keep the edge on their marriage love, Puritan writers offer practical advice: Gouge, for example, tells us that "*outward mutual peace*" is "one of the principall ... means of maintaining an inward loving affection betwixt Man and Wife"; they should therefore "avoid offence"; if it is given, they should pass it by: "Let them suffer their own will to be crossed, rather than discontent be given to the other." If both be incensed together, "offer reconciliation"; if it is offered, accept it. Do not bring "children, servants," or others "in the family" into your frays. Do not compare your spouse to another. "Bee not jealous. Endavour to please one another." Counseling husbands, Baxter says, "Make not the infirmities" of your wives "to seem *odious faults*, but excuse them as far as you lawfully may, by considering the frailty of the Sex ... and considering also your *own* infirmities, and how much your *Wives* must bear with you."[72]

Like the sharpening of a knife, however, the Puritan's advice on cultivating marriage love tends to be superficial, inadequate to the task of enabling us to be husbands and wives who are the deepest of lovers and the best of friends. For the demands upon us are very high in this idea of marriage, even when we are married to someone to whom we are temperamentally suited. Not many of us find it easy to achieve what the Puritans say we must. There are many reasons for this; I shall note two rather general ones: first, there is in many of us, a great deal of mistrust and fear of those we love or want to love; often there is a great deal of anger and defensiveness towards them as well. At least in part, these attitudes have their source in our experience of our own family when we were children; this past makes it difficult for us, as spouses, to nourish and maintain the required love of our husbands or wives. In addition, those we love, or seek to love, may have a similar mistrust or fear. They thus may not find it easy to accept, indeed, may actively discourage, our expressions of love and affection.

Such fears and defensiveness are not easily gotten at through the means the Puritans advise us to use. Beyond this, their notion that wives ought to forego expressions of anger hardly seems appropriate to a marriage in which wives as well as husbands are to receive deep forms of comfort and support from their partners. Anger is a natural occurrence from time to time in any close relation; if we repeatedly ignore it believing we ought to be docile, it does not thereby go away, at least not in ordinary cases, but reveals itself in a variety of ways; for example, in a generally bad temper, pervasive coldness, or loss of interest.

Moreover, the Puritans' emphasis on the unique friendship of marriage poses problems. They call upon husband and wife to be the best of friends, but they do not call upon each spouse to have close and intense friendships with anyone else. This is unwise. Perhaps our spouse should be our best friend, and the only one with whom we have sex, but it is difficult to develop a friendship and sustain it, if all our (emotional) eggs are in one basket. The Penalty we pay if our trust is misplaced is too great, for we have no one to turn to if our best friend, our husband or wife, fails us in some way: no one to turn to but the very source of our sorrow. It is *possible* to nourish a friendship on this basis, but it seems to me difficult.

These difficulties can be removed. Husbands and wives can give up the notion that men must rule and women submit. We can develop strong friendships with others, so that there will be others to whom we can turn in times of marriage trouble. But there are more general difficulties which remain. We cannot easily heal the psychic wounds that disable us from loving our spouses, or accepting their love, for these injuries lie deep. They are found in parts of our psyche that do not commonly respond to sage words of advice, nor are they removed by the peremptory demands of conscience.

We might therefore conclude that the Puritan demands are impossibly high, since very many of us cannot fulfill the duties of marriage they describe without a deep personal transformation that is surely not to be accomplished by following the kind of advice they give to spouses who don't come up to snuff. But the Puritan conceptions of marriage have *not* died out; my own impression is that they are very much alive in the United States. It is a commonplace of nineteenth- and twentieth-century America that the family is supposed to be a haven in a heartless world, an island of ease and sweetness in the midst of an unforgiving world of commerce and industry, an oasis away from the "work ethic." For many of us, perhaps, it has been the other way around: doing well in business is *easy* compared to what is expected of us at home. Perhaps this is why some of us work so hard: we can do so much better in career than we can do at home, where the claims of intimacy, friendship, and true love loom so large. Work is a haven from a home asking more than our hearts, or our spouses' hearts, can give.

Perhaps Puritan notions of marriage also account for some of the popularity of psychoanalysis and allied therapies in this country during the last half-century, for in the American context, these therapies have held out the promise of enabling men and women to meet the demands of marriage (or similar non-legal relations) more successfully.[73] It is curious that American psychotherapy, so often seen as hostile to "puritanism," in fact often serves this Puritan end. Indeed, for some, therapy becomes the test of whether a marriage is to continue or not.[74] If a marriage is in trouble, one or both spouses seek therapy; if, after due time, they still cannot provide each other with the needed warmth and comfort, then they think a divorce justified. For they believe that nothing more can be done. The temperamental failings lie too deep to be cured.

In retrospect, it appears that the Puritan demands upon spouses were not matched by the means which they gave to married couples to meet these demands. A similar situation may be still true today. Nonetheless, we might attribute at least some of the popularity of psychotherapies in the United States to their ability (or presumed ability) to make us what we should be as husbands and wives. In any case, if we want to look at the sources of some of the present perplexities of marriage, we had better not look only at Locke, but at Gouge, Gataker, Rogers, and their colleagues. The Puritans were fanatic about many things, including marriage; at least in this area, many of us continue a devotion to their demands, although we are not so sure about how well we are able to meet them.

NOTES

Two texts stand out as insightful introductions to Puritan theories of marriage: Levin Ludwig Schucking, *Die Puritanische Families in literarsoziologischer Sicht* (Berne and Munich: Francke Verlag, 1964, eng. trans., 1969), and William Haller and Malleville Haller, "The Puritan Art of Love," *Huntington Library Quarterly* 5 (1941–42):235–272. For criticisms of the claim of Schucking (and others) that Puritan views on marriage were novel, see Margo Todd, "Humanists, Puritans and the Spiritualized Household," *Church History* 49 (1980):18–34, and Kathleen M. Davies, "The Sacred Condition of Equality—How Original Were Puritan Doctrines of Marriage?" *Social History* 2 (1977):563–580.

1. Those who were Puritan in the ways described divided on the details of their ethics, belief, rite, and piety, and on other matters as well. The legitimacy of clerical authority and, more generally, of all hierarchies of wealth and power was a great point of contention. For an interesting discussion of this issue at the end of the Interregnum, see Barry Reay, "The Quakers, 1659, and The Restoration of the Monarchy," *History* 63 (1978):193–213. For a discussion of the meaning of "Puritan" in the sixteenth and seventeenth centuries, see Basil Hall, "Puritanism: The Problem of Definition," in, *Studies in Church History* 2, ed. by G. J. Cuming (London: Nelson, 1965), pp. 283–296. Much too can be learned from Vytautas Kavolis, "Social Movements and Civilizational Processes," *Comparative Civilizations Review* 8 (1982):31–58.

2. Roman Catechism of 1566, pp. 2, 8, 13, 14, in, John Thomas Noonan, *Contraception* (Cambridge: Harvard University Press, 1965).

3. In De Bono Conjugale (3. 3), Augustine writes that the marriage of old people must have some other purpose than procreation: it is the good of "mutual companionship between the two sexes" (*in diversu sexu societatem*). This notion of companionship as a good is omitted, however, in his general statements in this work concerning the good of marriage. See Noonan, *Contraception*, p. 128.

4. It lives, too, in Noonan, *Contraception*, an excellent and subtle work.

5. John Major (1519):4. 31, in Noonan, *Contraception*, p. 311.

6. Noonan, *Contraception*, p. 326.

7. Noonan, p. 276.

8. Erasmus of Rotterdam, *A Right Frutefull Epystle . . . in Laude and Prayse of Matrymony*, tr. of *Encomium matrimonii* by Richard Tavernour (London: R. Redman, 1530, 1st pub. in Latin, 1518).

9. Erasmus, *A Right Frutefull Epystle*, sigs. A5^v-[A7^r]. Although first published in printed form on March 30, 1518, Telle says that "en fait la publication de l'*Encomium Matrimonii* ne date pas de mars 1518," for in some form or other, "l'opuscule était connu en manuscrit depuis plus de vingt ans et courait de mains en mains à travers toute l'Europe." Emile Telle, *Erasme de Rotterdam et le septième sacrement* (Geneva: E. Droz, 1954), p. 155.

10. Erasmus, *A Right Frutefull Epystle*, sig. A3^r. Even the English do, says Erasmus, in Telle, *Erasme*, p. 165, but Tavernour does not include this wisecrack in his translation. Telle, in *Erasme*, p. 165 (n. 28) and pp. 179–180, thinks that this passage suggests that the *Encomium* "a été remanié en Angleterre au contact du groupe Colet, Latimer, Linacre, More. En cette fin de XVe et debut de XVIe siecle, il appert que la question du mariage était un des sujets les plus debattus outre-Manche. . . . C'est dans ce pays où la question du celibat, du mariage et surtout des mauvais mariages parait avoir été à l'ordre du jour." For the evidence which

Telle offers for the English influence on Erasmus' views on marriage, see esp. *Erasme*, pp. 197–180.

11. "Humanists, Puritans and the Spiritualized Household," pp. 18, 21.

12. Todd, p. 32.

13. Telle, *Erasme*, p. 462.

14. Robert Bellarmine, *An Ample Declaration of the Christian Doctrine*, tr. by Richard Hadock (Douai, 1604), pp. 257–58. Telle (p. 458) thinks that Erasmus works out his anti-celibatarian views in terms of "le paulisme matrimonial," but provides plenty of evidence to link them to a philosophy of what is natural and proper to humankind that is alive in Aristotle, Thomas, the late medieval theologians I mention above, as well as the humanists, Italian and Northern. Telle (p. 180) writes that Erasmus "n'a jamais écrit ni pensé cette phrase par exemple [:] 'Quod naturae est, imputatur a malo'." Would this be any less true of Thomas?

15. See note 10 above.

16. Todd, "Humanists, Puritans and the Spiritualized Household," p. 19.

17. Daniel Rogers, *Matrimoniall Honour* (London: Philip Nevil, 1642), p. 9.

18. William Gouge, *Of Domesticall Duties*, 2nd ed. (London: John Beale, 1626), pp. 242, 123. Jeremy Taylor, *The Rule and Exercises of Holy Living*, 2nd ed. (London: Richard Royston, 1657), pp. 81–82, disagrees with the Puritans on this point. In his estimation of celibacy, he is close to Bellarmine. He praises a chaste widowhood, but reserves his highest esteem for the virginal life: It is "a life of Angels": "being unmingled with the world, it is apt to converse with God: and by not feeling the warmth of a too forward and indulgent nature, flames out with Holy fires, till it be burned like the Cherubin . . . Natural virginity of itself is not a state more acceptable to God: but that which is chosen and voluntary in order to the conveniences of Religion and separation from worldly incumbrances, is therefore better than the married life; . . . it is a freedom from cares, an opportunity to spend more time in spiritual imployment; . . . it containeth in it a victory over lusts, and great desires of Religion and self-denial, and therefore is more excellent than the married life." It allows as Taylor says elsewhere, "a perfect mortification of our strongest appetites" (in *Eniatos*, 2nd ed., 2 vols. [London: Richard Royston, 1655], p. 222).

Self-mortification is a well-developed theme in both the Puritan and Roman Catholic worlds of the sixteenth and seventeenth centuries, but the Puritans do not make much of self-mortification through the denial of the sexuality which belongs to marriage love, a love both spiritual and yet sensual, a love which leads couples to marry and sustains them once married. For this reason, Max Weber's characterization of Puritanism as an "inner-worldly asceticism" is misleading. The Puritans *do* call for mortification of sexual desire when illicit, but they call for an *integration* of the sexuality of *husband and wife* with other elements of the good and holy life. They therefore reject the admiration of sexual self-mortification found in the Roman Church of the sixteenth and seventeenth centuries, for example, in authors as different as Ignatius of Loyola and Pascal. Weber is plainly wrong when he writes that "the sexual asceticism of Puritanism differs only in degree, not in fundamental principle," from that of Western medieval monasticism. (See Max Weber, *Gesammelte Aufsätze zur Religionssoziologie*, Vol. I [Tubingen: J. C. B. Mohr, 1920], pp. 169–170; English translation, *The Protestant Ethic and the Spirit of Capitalism*, tr. by T. Parsons [New York: Scribner, 1958], p. 158.) In this matter, the case of Baxter is instructive. Unlike most of the Puritans who wrote about marriage, and in spite of the spiritual support he received from his life, he thought the single life generally more suitable to the main ends of the Christian life. These ends are three: to "serve God," advance our "spiritual welfare," and increase our "Holinesse." Yet he does not praise those who choose the chaste single life for their sexual renunciation, nor does he list the sexual aspect of marriage as one of its spiritual disadvantages. In the main, his objection is that marriage creates so many worldly cares and concerns that it easily impedes both the active and contemplative elements of the Christian life, a theme well-known in the writings of the Roman Church, but linked in that tradition to an admiration of sexual renunciation. See Baxter, *A Christian Directory*, II, pp. 3–12.

19. Gouge, *Of Domesticall Duties*, I, p. 123. William Ames, *Conscience with the Power and Cases Thereof* (London, 1639), p. 197. Daniel Rogers, *Matrimoniall Honour* (London: Philip Nevil, 1642), p. 6. Secker writes, "One of the Popes of *Rome*, sprinkles this unholy drop" upon marriage: "*carnis polutionem & immunditem*." "It's strange," says Secker, "that that should be a pollution, which was instituted before corruption: or that impurity, which was ordained in the state of innocency," in, William Secker, *A Wedding Ring Fit for the Finger* (London: Thomas Parkhurst, 1658), p. 17.

20. Secker, *A Wedding Wing*, p. 15.

21. Gouge, *Of Domesticall Duties*, I, p. 121.

22. Gouge, *Of Domesticall Duties*, p. 131. Baxter, *A Christian Directory*, II, p. 40. Rogers, *Matrimoniall Honour*, p. 146.

23. Thomas Gataker, *A Mariage Praier* (London: Fulke Clifton and James Bowler, 1624), p. 146.

24. Taylor, *Eniatos*, II, pp. 224–225.

25. Baxter, *A Christian Directory*, II, p. 41.

26. Thomas Gataker, *Marriage Duties Briefly Couched Togither* (London: William Bladen, 1620), p. 37.

27. Rogers, *Matrimoniall Honour*, p. 150.

28. Baxter, *A Christian Directory*, II, p. 42. Gataker, *Marriage Duties*, p. 44.

29. For a similar use of this passage, see Matthew Griffith, *Bethel: or, a Forme for Families* (London: Ro. Allott and Hen. Taunton, 1634), pp. 280–281, 286, and Baxter, *A Christian Directory*, II, p. 42.

30. Baxter, *A Christian Directory*, II, p. 43.

31. Gataker, *Marriage Duties*, p. 37. For similar remarks, see Gouge, *Of Domesticall Duties*, pp. 239–241.

32. Gataker, *Marriage Duties*, p. 44; and Gouge, *Of Domesticall Duties*, p. 134.

33. Rogers, *Matrimoniall Honour*, p. 157. Gouge, *Of Domesticall Duties*, p. 208. For a like passage, see Gataker, *Marriage Duties*, p. 44. Lucy, wife of a Puritan soldier, herself a Puritan, and brought up in a Puritan household, begins her description of the physical appearance of her late husband in the following way, in a memoir of him prepared for the benefit of their children: "He was of middle stature, of a slender and exactly well-proportioned shape in all parts, his complexion fair, his hair of light brown, very thick set in his youth, softer than the finest silk, and curling into loose great rings at the ends; his eyes of a lively grey, well-shaped and full of life and vigour, graced with many becoming motions; his visage thin, his mouth well made, his lips very ruddy and graceful, although the nether chap shut over the upper, yet it was in such a manner as was not unbecoming; his teeth were even and white as the purest ivory, his chin was something long, and the mould of his face; his forehead was not very high; his nose was raised and sharp; but withal he had a most amiable countenance, which carried in it something of magnanimity and majesty mixed with sweetness, that at the same time bespoke love and awe in all that saw him; his skin was smooth and white, his legs and feet excellently well-made; he was quick in his pace and turns, nimble and active and graceful in all his motions; he was apt for any bodily excercise, and any that he did became him; he could dance admirably well, but neither in youth nor riper years made any practice of it . . . " She goes on to describe other admirable qualities, including those he possessed in music, dress, and wit. A separate and major section of her memoir is devoted to his moral and spiritual virtues.

Her description of her husband, no doubt, owes much to modes of thought and perception that do not have their *origins* in Puritan culture. She is familiar with elements of the culture of the court, which owed much to the aristocratic manners and arts of the Continent. Her father was a gentleman who had spent time at court; she herself grew up in the precincts of the Tower of London, "whereof her father" had been "made lieutenant." In, Lucy Hutchinson, *Memoirs of Colonel Hutchinson* (London: Dent, 1965), p. 10.

She writes of herself as a child, "I thought it no sin to learn or hear witty songs and amorous sonnets or poems, and twenty things of that kind, wherein I was so apt that I became the confidant in all the loves that were managed among my mother's young women" (p. 15). These sonnets or poems were not of Puritan origin, yet they were shared and sung in a Puritan household; as a grown woman, she disapproves of them, yet her own description shows that when she seeks to express her love of *her husband*, she still favors that amorous style learned in her youth.

The literature of knightly romance—*Amadis of Gaul* and the like—so popular in Elizabethan and Stuart England, even among the pious, also taught the Puritans something about the passion of love. To assuage the conscience of the pious reader, the stories were often given a moral veneer. Such literature is less in evidence in seventeenth-century New England, though it is by no means absent: see. Louis Booker Wright, *Middle-Class Culture in Elizabethan England* (Chapel Hill: University of North Carolina Press, 1953), and *The Cultural Life of the American Colonies*, 1607–1763 (New York: Harper, 1957), pp. 141–144. For an amusing use of the literary style of the romance in early eighteenth-century New England, see the journal of Sarah Kemble Knight first published in 1825; for a twentieth-century edition, see Sarah Kemble Knight, *The Journal of Madam Knight*, ed. by Malcolm Freiberg (Boston: David R. Godine, 1972). A lively excerpt is published in Perry Miller and Thomas J. Johnson, eds. *The Puritans* (New York: Harper & Row, 1963), II, pp. 425–447.

The literature of romance, as developed in the more refined forms of English poetry, may have also played a part in encouraging the flowering of romantic notions of marriage love among the Puritans. John Leverett, later to be president of Harvard College, while still a student, copied out several stanzas from Cowley's "Elegie upon Anacreon" and "The Mistress." Elnathan Chauncy, son of Harvard's President Charles Chauncy, copied out lyrics of both Herrick, including most of "Gather ye rosebuds while ye may," and Spenser; he gave twenty pages of his notebook to the latter poet; see Samuel Eliot Morison, *The Puritan Pronaos* (New York: New York University Press, 1936), pp. 46–52. Milton was not the only Puritan who read Spenser.

For the Spenserian background of Milton's thoughts on marriage love, see William Haller, "Hail Wedded Love'." *ELH* 13 (1946):76–97. For a complex and sophisticated discussion of ideas of marriage, love, and sexuality in Spenser and in Shakespeare, see Walter B. C. Watkins, *Shakespeare and Spenser* (Princeton: Princeton University Press, 1950).

34. Puritan writers often turned to the Song of Songs to illustrate the love that a husband must have for a wife, and a wife for a husband, as the Hallers have noted, in, William Haller and Malleville Haller, "The Puritan Art of Love," p. 243. See, above all, Rogers, *Matrimoniall Honour*, p. 313. Also, William Perkins, *Christian Oeconomis*, Vol. III in *Workes* (London: John Legatt et al., 1616–1618), II, p. 691; Gouge; Griffith, p. 289; and John Milton, *Tetrachordon*, 1645, p. 335. For further documentation of the place of sexual love in marriage, as it is seen by Puritans who affirm its place in no uncertain terms, see Roland Mushat Frye, "The Teachings of Classical Puritanism on Conjugal Love," in, *Studies in the Renaissance*, 2, ed. by M. A. Shaber (New York: The Renaissance Society of America, 1955).

Not all Puritans emphasize the sexual and sensual delight of marriage love. William Perkins does not make much of it. True, he says that "the Communion of man and wife" is a duty which "consisteth principally in the performance of speciall benevolence to one another, and that not of courtesie, but of due debt." Spouses must show "a singular and entire affection towards one another." among other ways, "by an holy kind of rejoycing and solacing themselves with each other, in a mutual declaration of the signes and tokens of love and kindness." To support his position, he quotes, in addition to *Proverbs* 5: 18, 19, *Song of Songs* 1. 1: "*Let him kiss mee with the kisses of his mouth, for thy love is better than wine.*" On the other hand, Perkins does not say anything of this joyous, and sensuous intimacy in his discussion of the ends of marriage, though he does say that mutual comfort is one of them, in, Perkins, *Christian Oeconomie*, III, pp. 689, 691, 671.

Baxter, too, fails to make much of the sensual and sexual side of marriage. He does tell husband and wife that they must take delight in each other; he adds the comment that men are perverse enough to turn "the *lawful delight* allowed them by God . . . into loathing and disdain." This, they must not do: *Proverbs* 5: 18–19 must be their guide, in, Baxter, *A Christian Directory*, II, p. 42. Yet he does not make the mutual delights and comforts of marriage a chief reason to marry. We must marry if we can serve God and ourselves better by doing so; we must marry if our parents require it of us (and there is "*no greater matter* on the contrary to hinder it"); we must marry if we are free to do so and "have not the gift of *Continence.*" The good of mutual support and comfort comes in by the back door, in answer to the question, "*May the aged marry that are frigid, Impotent, and uncapable of procreation? Answ.* Yes, God hath not forbidden them: And there are other lawful ends of marriage, as mutual help and comfort &c. which may make it lawful" in, Baxter, II, pp. 3–4. It takes a question about *the aged* to make him mention comfort as reason for marriage; he does not think that they are that interested in sexual delight: he quotes Bacon, who says that wives are "old mens nurses"—a good enough reason for an elderly man to marry. Baxter was less willing than others to integrate the sexual with the affective, ethical and even spiritual elements of marriage.

With respect to sexuality in marriage, Baxter is thus sometimes close to the anonymous author of *The Practice of Christian Graces or The Whole Duty of Man* (1659), pp. 168–169 (quoted in Schucking, *Die Puritanische Families in literarsoziologischer Sicht,* p. 23), an enormously popular guide to conduct in late seventeenth-century England, the England of the Restoration. This author writes that in "lawful marriage . . . men are not to think themselves let loose to please their brutish appetites, but are to keep themselves within such rules of moderation, as agree to the ends of Marriage, which [are] . . . the begetting of children, and the avoiding of fornication."

The character of Baxter's thought and feeling perhaps misled Weber in his judgment of Puritanism, for the sociologist takes Baxter as an exemplar of Puritan attitudes toward marriage sexuality. Perhaps this is why Weber thinks that modern dissociations of sexuality from the deeper dimensions of emotional life are congenial to the Puritan sensibility. For the fortunate, Weber thinks, there exists, beyond the realm of reason and cultural demands, a life of desire, love, and passion, tragic in its irrationality, yet profoundly sustaining in its meaning. He abhorred the "moderns" of his time who had no inkling of this darkly luminous realm, who made sexuality a merely medical, physiological, or hygienic phenomenon: a purely "rational" matter.

Writing of his own time, Weber remarks that "in a lecture, a zealous adherent of hygienic prostitution—it was a question of the regulation of brothels and prostitutes—defended the moral legitimacy of extra-marital intercourse (which was looked upon as hygienically useful) by referring to its poetic justification in the case of Faust and Margaret." Weber comments: "To treat Margaret as a prostitute and to fail to distinguish the powerful sway of human passion from sexual intercourse for hygienic reasons, both are thoroughly congenial to the Puritan standpoint," in Weber, *Gesammelte Aufsätze,* I, p. 170, n. 1; *Protestant Ethic,* pp. 263–64). Weber, is mistaken; the Puritans understood and even sanctified the passionate desire and erotic longing for another which endowed the Puritan marriage bed with life-meanings far deeper than those captured by physiology. In marriage love, with its sexuality, we find a true friend and companion, a second self: we are redeemed from our loneliness. The Puritans would have condemned the love that joined Gretchen and Faust together, but they call for a love, *within marriage*, no less deep and no less passionate.

The "hygienic" view which Weber abhors was perhaps the outlook of Bertrand Russell's mother and father. In his autobiography (Bertrand Russell, *Autobiography*, 3 Vols. [Boston: Little, Brown and Company, 1967–1969], I, p. 10), Russell writes that his parents obtained for his brother "a tutor of some scientific ability," who was, however, "in an advanced state of consumption." "Apparently upon grounds of pure theory, my father and mother decided that although he ought to remain childless on account of tuberculosis, it was unfair to expect him to be celibate. My mother therefore allowed him to live with her, though I know of no evidence that she derived any pleasure from doing so."

35. Baxter, *A Christian Directory*, II, p. 44.

36. Baxter, *A Christian Directory*, II, pp. 18–31. Gouge, *Of Domesticall Duties*, pp. 138–139.

37. Richard Baxter, *A Breviate of the Life of Margaret, the Daughter of Francis Charlton . . . and Wife of Richard Baxter* (London: B. Simmons and Brabazon Aylmer, 1681), pp. 70–71.

38. Gataker, *Marriage Duties*, p. 1.

39. See, for example, Rogers, *Matrimoniall Honour*, pp. 211, 304–306. See Gataker, *A Marriage Praier*, p. 20, in which Gataker quotes from I Peter 3.4: "*A Meeke and quiet spirit, in a woman especially, is a thing*, saith *Saint Peter, much set by in Gods sight*." And also see Ames, *Conscience with the Power and the Cases Thereof*, p. 156 and Rogers, *Matrimoniall Honour*, pp. 236–253.

40. See Rogers, *Matrimoniall Honour*, p. 220, who quotes Paul (I Timothy 5.8): "He that provides not for his family hath forsaken the faith, and is worse than an Infidell." For Rogers' extended reproof of improvident husbands, whom he divides into nine sorts, see pp. 230–236. For the wife, see Rogers, pp. 288–296.

41. Gataker, *A Mariage Praier*, pp. 18–19.

42. Baxter, in *A Breviate*, p. 67, writes that he "never knew" the "equal" of his wife's reason in "*prudential practical*" matters: "in very hard cases, about what was to be done, she would suddenly open all the way that was to be opened, in things of the Family, Estate, or any civil business. And to confess the truth, experience acquainted her, that I knew less in such things than she; and therefore was willing she should take it all upon her."

43. Jeremy Taylor, *The Measures and Offices of Friendship*, 3rd ed. (London: R. Royston, 1662), pp. 79–83. Ames, in *Conscience* (1639), tells us that a husband "ought to reckon of his Wife in all things, as his neerest Companion, and as part of himselfe, or of the same whole, in a certaine parity of honour."

44. In answer to a letter from Appius Claudius Pulcher, who has just returned to Rome, Cicero (*Ad Familiares* 3. 9. 1) writes, "At last, after all, I have read a letter worthy of Appius Claudius—a letter full of kindly feeling, courtesy, and consideration [*plenas humanitatis, offici, diligentiae*]. Evidently the very sight of your urban surroundings has given you back your pristine urbanity." Brunt (" 'Amicitia' in the Late Roman Republic," *Proceedings of the Cambridge Philological Society* 191, ii [1965]:1–20) writes that "*sermo*" [conversation], "*litterae*" [letters, in the broad sense], and "*humanitas*" were recognised in Cicero's Rome "as qualities which might make even a disreputable man a welcome associate on whom the name of friend could be bestowed."

45. Taylor, *The Measures and Offices of Friendship*, pp. 29–31.

46. Michel de Montaigne, *Complete Essays*, tr. by Donald M. Frame (Stanford: Stanford University Press, 1958), pp. 136–137 (from *Essais*, I, 28 [*De l'amitié*]).

47. Thus, for Martial, the difficulty of gaining a woman makes her attractive; there must be some difficulty, else no desire can arise:

Moechus es Aufidiae, qui vir, Scaevine, fruisti;
   rivalis fuerat qui tuus, ille vir est.
cur aliena placet tibi, quae tua non placet, uxor?
   numquid securus non potes arrigere? (*Epigrams* 3. 70)

In Ker's translation (Martial, *Epigrams*, tr. by W. C. A. Ker, 2 Vols. [London: William Heinemann, 1919]):

You are the paramour of Aufidia, and you were Scaevinus, her husband; he who was your rival is her husband. Why does another man's wife please you when she as your own does not please you? Is it that when secure you lack appetite?

For further examples of the same strain of thought in the *Epigrams*, see 1. 57 and 1. 73.

48. Montaigne, *Complete Essays*, p. 138 (*Essais*, I, 28).

49. For a recent edition, written after her husband's death in 1664, but not published until 1806, see Lucy Hutchinson, *Memoirs of Colonel Hutchinson*, 1965.

50. Benjamin Nelson, *The Idea of Usury*, 2nd ed. (Chicago: University of Chicago Press, 1969), pp. 139–164.

51. Martin Luther, *Von Kaufshandlung und Wucher*, 1524, quoted in Nelson, p. 152.

52. Walter Raleigh, *Works*, 2 Vols (London, 1751), II, pp. 351–352; quoted in Nelson, pp. 147–148.

53. Benjamin Nelson, "*Eros, Logos, Nomos, Polis*: Their Changing Balances and The Vicissitudes of Communities and Civilizations," in, *Changing Perspectives in the Scientific Study of Religion*, ed. by Alan W. Eister (New York: Wiley-Interscience, 1974), pp. 85–111.

54. A careful reading of Locke's statements on marriage is found in Mary Lyndon Shanley, "Marriage Contract and Social Contract in Seventeenth Century Political Thought," *Western Political Quarterly* 32 (1979):79–91. For one Puritan discussion of marriage as a contracts, see Rogers, *Matrimoniall Honour*, pp. 96–126.

55. John Locke, *Two Treatises of Government*, ed. by Peter Laslett (New York: New American Library, 1963), II, 79, 82. I quote from Peter Laslett's edition of the Treatises which is based on the third printing (1968), as corrected by Locke. "I" and "II" indicate the *First* and *Second Treatises* respectively. I refer to the sections of the Treatises, rather than to pages of Laslett's edition, for the convenience of readers who use other editions.

56. Locke, *Treatises*, II, 81. Locke's view is a version of an argument rejected by the young Thomas Aquinas in his commentary on the sentences of Peter Lombard (*Scriptum in IV Libros Sententiarum* 4. 33. 2. 1). "The union of man and woman in marriage is chiefly directed to the begetting, rearing, and instruction of offspring. But all things are complete by a certain time. Therefore after that time it is lawful to put away a wife without prejudice to the natural law." Thomas replies, "By the intention of nature marriage is directed to the rearing of offspring, not merely for a time, but throughout its whole life. Hence it is of natural law that parents should lay up for their children, and that children should be their parents' heirs." Because sustaining the welfare of children is not a limited task of marriage, but a permanent one, husband and wife "must live together for ever inseparably." Different notions of the obligations of parents to their grown children divide Thomas and Locke. For Thomas, the solidarity of the family unit remains crucial to the welfare of grown children; therefore, the marriage of their parents is not to be dissolved. The same point can be sustained by an examination of some of Thomas' arguments for the indissolubility of marriage in the *Summa Contra Gentiles* (3. 123). The strain of individualism in Locke's thought surfaces in his unwillingness to have parents bound by obligations to their children throughout their whole lives: just as children must become free of parents, so parents must become free of

children. The realities of English life, in Locke's time, however, often made grown children of the better classes very much dependent upon their parents' good will.

57. John Locke, *Journal*, 1679, Locke MSS (Oxford: Bodleian), quoted in Locke, *Treatises*, p. 364, note to 81.

58. James Turner Johnson, *A Society Ordered by God; English Puritan Marriage Doctrines in the First Half of the Seventeenth Century* (Nashville: Abingdon Press, 1970).

59. John Milton, *The Doctrine and Discipline of Divorce*, 2nd ed. (London, 1664). *Tetrachordon*, 1645). *Colasterion* (London, 1645). See Milton's edition of Bucer's work on divorce, in, Martin Bucer, *The Judgement of Martin Bucer, Concerning Divorce*, tr. by John Milton (London: Matthew Simmons, 1644). Also see Haller and Haller, "The Puritan Art of Love," and Haller, " 'Hail Wedded Love'."

60. Locke, *Treatises*, II, 82.

61. Weber, *The Protestant Ethic*, pp. 166–167 (*Gesammelte*, I, p. 183).

62. Weber, *Gesammelte*, I, p. 116; English translation which I have slightly modified, pp. 118–119.

63. Weber, *Gesammelte*, I, p. 118; English translation, p. 119.

64. On "integration" as a formative principle of the Puritan personality, see Zevedei Barbu, *Problems of Historical Psychology* (New York: Grove Press, 1960).

65. The conviction that we must choose between erotic self-expression and rational discipline is well expressed in *Die Strasse* (1923), *Die Freudlose Gasse* (1925), "street films" of the 1920s, as well as in *Der Blaue Engel* (1930). After the Second World War, that same theme runs through *Das Madchen Rosemarie* (1958). On the movies of the 1920s and 30s, especially the street movies, see Siegfried Kracauer, *From Caligari to Hitler* (Princeton: Princeton University Press, 1947).

66. Weber, *Gesammelte*, I, p. 563; English translation in *From Max Weber: Essays in Sociology*, tr. and ed. by H. H. Gerth and C. Wright Mills (New York: Oxford University Press, 1946), p. 350.

67. Rogers, *Matrimoniall Honour*, pp. 147–148.

68. Thomas Gataker, *A Good Wife Gods Gift* (London: Fulke Clifton, 1623).

69. Baxter, *A Christian Directory*, II, p. 12 writes, "*Next to the fear of God* make choice of a *nature, or temperament that is not too much unsuitable to you*. A crossness of Dispositions will be a continued vexation: and you will have a Domestick War instead of Love." Yet he would not praise, as Rogers does, the mysterious source of the love of a man and a woman which leads them to wed: "*Take special care, that fansie and passion over-rule not Reason*, and *Friends advice in the choice . . . of the person* [you marry]. I know you must have Love to those you match with: But that *Love* must be *Rational*, and such as you can justifie in the severest trial, by the evidences of *worth* and *fitness* in the person whom you love. To say *you Love*, but you *know not why*, is more beseeming Children or mad folks, than those that are soberly entering upon a change of so great importance to them" (II, 10).

70. I am indebted to conversations with Robert Merrihew Adams for the perception of this central element of Puritan moral theology. It should not be supposed that the Puritans held this view just in order to make us acutely aware of the unavoidable impurity and sinfulness of our hearts and wills, in the hope of bringing us to a real sense of our need for salvation through God's grace and Christ's redemptive act. On the contrary, it would make more sense to say that it was because of their belief that "ought" need not imply "can" that many Puritans had such an acute sense of sin.

71. The Puritan casuists, Milton excepted, thought that although temperamental affinity was of prime importance in the choice of a partner, a man had no right to divorce because he made a bad choice; see Gataker, *Marriage Duties*, p. 35. Milton went a daring step further.

72. Rogers, *Matrimoniall Honour*, p. 156. Gouge, *Of Domesticall Duties*, pp. 133–134. Baxter, *A Christian Directory*, II, p. 41. Puritans sometimes say that if you are unfortunate enough to choose a mate that does not suit your temperament, you must strive to achieve what is beyond human power: you must bring yourself to love, by dint of effort and reason, a spouse that does not suit you. Gataker, in, *A Good Wife Gods Gift* (London: Fulker Clifton, 1623), p. 11 and *Marriage Duties*, p. 35, speaking of the choice of a mate, says that "there are secret links of affection, that no reason can be rendered of: as there are inbred dislikes, that neither can be resolved, nor reconciled." "As there is no affection more forcible: than love, "so there is none freer from force and compulsion." He quotes Cassiodorus: "*Amor non cogitur.*" Yet he tells those who have married one they cannot love "to strive even to enforce their affections; and crave grace at Gods hand, where by they may be enabled to bring themselves to that disposition, that God now requireth."

73. For solid evidence of this see Nathan G. Hale, Jr., "From Berggasse XIX to Central Park West: The Americanization of Psychoanalysis, 1919–1940," *Journal of the History of the Behavioral Sciences* 14 (1978):299–315.

74. This was pointed out to me by my father, Nathan Leites, in a conversation which took place in a Moroccan restaurant on (I believe) the Boulevard St. Germain in 1977.

10. The Games of Life and the Dances of Death

Benjamin Nelson

A premier Poet of our time once sang:

> *This is the way the world ends*
> *This is the way the world ends*
> *This is the way the world ends*
> *Not with a bang but a whimper.*[1]

The Poet would almost certainly have been mistaken had he meant his remarks to apply to civilizations. Civilizations do not end with a *bang* or a *whimper*. Civilizations generally die laughing!

The more closely great societies approach the point of checkmate, the deeper the indulgence of great numbers in their favorite games. In fact, the worse the situation, the more hectic the abandonment. It is when all is fun and joy, on the go-go, when the dancers in the charades are at the edge of ecstasy and frenzy, that the hoped-for oblivion prevails. At this juncture, treasured elements of the legacy of civilizations slip unnoticed out of focus.[2]

Abundant evidence for these statements is available to those students of history and sociology who attend strongly to the ways in which the classes and the masses alike have related to certain of the very critical transitions in their histories. The more closely we study the episodes, the more we discover that relatively few can sense or understand the changes which occur in peak structures of value or in all of those sensibilities which might have had to be maintained if civilizations are somehow to be preserved.

The depictions by Samuel Dill and others of Roman society of the late fourth and fifth centuries A.D.[3] tell the story eloquently. The available evidence on political and economic developments makes it clear that the Imperial Establishment was sagging. In losing to the Visigoths at

Adrianople (A.D. 378), the Romans had suffered a crucial break in their frontiers. Very decisive structures at every level appeared to be crumbling. Yet, when we read their letters and other literary efforts, we discover that only a handful of men cared to relate to the circumstances of their undoing.

Christian thinkers were, in the main, more prone to respond to the crisis than were the pagans. The reasons are easy enough to see. For St. Augustine, the sack of Rome in 410 offered the needed proof that the only true grounds for hope lay in the promise of a city uncontaminated by Rome's persisting corruptions, a city of God (*civitas Dei*).

But if we read the pagan letters of the time, we get a much more serene picture. We discover that long before the time of the worst onslaughts, the well-to-do had left the cities for country villas where they would regularly meet and engage one another in sports, charades of sociability, and polite banter about their literary traditions. How effete their favorite rhetoric was may be judged from stilted missives they wrote to one another from time to time. The situation continued to get worse, but the classes and for that matter the masses, neither truly understood nor cared to analyze their predicaments.[4]

Masses do not usually have the alternatives that the classes do. They cannot, for the most part, put things out of mind by devising genteel distractions. Masses are likely to be stirred into states of effervescence, to coalesce into collectivities and to move toward ways—whether political, prepolitical, or postpolitical—of achieving some new sense of vitality and existence. Masses often get to be completely involved in efforts to discover a collective oneness.

Patterns of this sort have occurred again and again. Sometimes a religion is formed in the midst of the effervescence; always there are powerful components goading men into mindlessness and into "trances of action." The reasons are not hard to find: the old ways have become tedious, everything that comes to mind in these times proves frightening. Rather than "minding," great numbers resort to drink, drugs, Dionysiac abandonment, disaster politics. No prejudice is intended in these words. A great deal of dying and being reborn is in process. This is one form of the equation of our essay.

There is another form of our equation which links the games of life men play in their hours of despair to their dances of death.[5] I begin with some paragraphs from Somerset Maugham's *Of Human Bondage*. Maugham is describing a Paris dance hall around 1900:

> The hall was lit by great white lights low down which emphasized the shadows on the faces, although the light seemed to harden under it and the colors were most curious. Philip leaned over the rails staring down. He ceased to hear the music. They danced

furiously. They danced around the room, slowly talking, but very little, with all their attention given to the dance. It seemed to Philip that they had thrown off the guard which people wear on their expression, and he saw them now as they really were. In that moment of abandon they were strangely animals. Some were foxy; some were wolf-life. Others had the long foolish faces of sheep. Their skins were sallow from the unhealthy life they led. Their features were blunted by mean interests and their little eyes were shifty and cunning. They were seeking escape from a world of horror.

Fate seemed to tower above them, and they danced as though everlasting darkness were about their feet. It was as if life terrified them, and the shriek that was in their hearts died within their throats. Notwithstanding the beastly lust which disfigured them and the meanness of their faces, and the cruelty. Notwithstanding the stupidity which was the worst of all, the anguish of these fixed eyes made all that crowd terrible and pathetic.[6]

Maugham's grim description locates the main elements of our scenario: the haste to stave off horror; the growing fascination with and the anguished flight from a sense of impending death; the experience of vertigo. It is against this background that men come to play their games of life.

A not so surprising effect occurs as the games grow more abandoned; the takeoff into oblivion accelerates. Played with enough frenzy, the games promise escape from the horrors of existence; precisely, then, the masks of the actors fall: *the games of life turn out to be dances of death.*

The equation I have just stated is one which has been very well understood by all those attuned to divining the signs of the times. Depictions of the agonies of interims recur throughout literature and art. My subsequent examples will be drawn mainly but not exclusively from the nineteenth and twentieth centuries.

In the arts, there are those who run ahead and who are especially sensitive to the quakes and tremors of their times. One such spiritual seismographer was Rimbaud, whose *Season in Hell* is a supreme illustration of the sorts of games that life suggests to those in the extremities of despair. Anyone wishing to have a more than superficial understanding of the twentieth century must come to know that Rimbaud's logbook offers us more insights into the profiles of our future sense of reality than myriad "futurological" publications which are now concerned with the Year 2000. Rimbaud was truly a visionary, one who saw far ahead in respect to the spiritual itineraries we would all encounter in our efforts to find our ways out of the maze.[7]

None of us ever really learns to live life. The living of death comes to us more or less naturally. We do not need to receive special lessons on how to live death. We move toward death with faultless ease and skill. Is this not exactly what many of our foremost playwrights, poets, and painters have been telling us? Among the playwrights I would mention only a few whose works make no sense unless they are read and experienced in the spirit of the equations I have been suggesting here.

Samuel Beckett's whole work is devoted to the notion that the boring charades which comprise our games of life are in their own little way *dances* on the way to a death—if, indeed, there is any reality to either life or death. Beckett never settles the question; we read him or listen to him in *Waiting for Godot*, in *Malone Dies*, and other plays and novels; we sense that he doesn't ever decide whether he is alive or dead or has yet been born. The whole of life has the quality of being a silly turn on the way to death, itself an illusory end to meaninglessness.[8]

The resistances men exhibit to facing the realities of their lives and deaths have provoked one playwright after another in our time. Audiences have worked wonders in fending off these messages. I recall the perplexities of more than one elegant and cultivated group when *The Iceman Cometh* of Eugene O'Neill first appeared on Broadway. In my naïveté, I originally supposed that everyone who saw or read the play would instantly recognize that *The Iceman Cometh* was a passion play. I found it the single most searing *contemporary* statement of this theme I had until then seen, relentlessly depicting the ways by which people seek to assure themselves that life eternal is theirs for the asking, exposing the "moonshine" and "pipedreams," everything—including the arts and sciences—which was fashioned in the attempt to make reality more bearable.

Those who remember the play cannot forget how stark were the alternatives with which O'Neill confronts us. As I was to learn only recently, O'Neill's stage directions directly recall the eve of the sacrifice of the paschal lamb. On Hickey's return to the saloon for the purpose of having a reunion with his old cronies, they throw themselves into having a wonderful time, living just as they always wanted to live and avoiding all the mess of the actual world. O'Neill's stage directions call upon Hickey and his cronies to be grouped in a manner which recalls Leonardo's painting of the Last Supper.[9] It turns out the "Last Supper" is not only with Christ but also with Freud. What O'Neill wants to argue is the proposition that neither Christ nor Freud will get us out of the "bum rap" of this living death.[10]

We must not be astonished that the disciples turn on Hickey-Christ-Freud. They wish to destroy him. In fact, they put him out of the way as hopelessly mad; what else could they do? Was he not telling them that the illusions they insisted upon living and reliving in this womb, that they had recreated for themselves, could not in the end suffice?

It is startling that I have not yet found the author or critic who has noticed that Hickey's old cronies set upon him exactly when he comes to deliver a message meant to bring them into close touch with reality. Are not those who come to deliver some message too hard for our ears, too strong for our hearts and minds, regularly set aside as being beside themselves? Who among us can look straight into the eyes of life and death?

Countless illustrations of the relationship between the games of life and the dances of death are found in major living playwrights, Sartre, Genet, Ionesco, Peter Weiss, and others less removed.

Most recently, the works of art which have spelled out our equation most profoundly are films, but for some reason, not easy to state in a formula, many critics of films seem to miss critical dimensions of what is happening. Too often in our day, we get psychoanalytic pathographies of the directors rather than interpretations of the film. A case in point is an essay which offers proof that Fellini's *Satyricon* illustrated Fellini's inability to shake his way free of the perversions and psychopathologies which consumed him. Was it not obvious that he had voyeuristic tendencies, that he was dedicated to sadistic perversion, that he had addictions to necrophilia, and so forth?

Are we prepared to overlook the fact that Fellini's most interesting and most recent pictures are located in Rome, the historic city of Rome? *La Dolce Vita*, which is certainly about Rome, has the nobility wandering through catacombs and old villas engaging in orgiastic, frenetic efforts to shake themselves free of agonizing obsessions of one kind or another. As many will recall, *La Dolce Vita* begins with a helicopter carrying aloft the image of Jesus.

When I first saw *La Dolce Vita,* I felt certain that Fellini's future work would have to include *The Satyricon.* Fellini had to film *Satyricon* because *Satyricon* was *our* story, spoke to *our* condition. Fellini's reputed perversions—his sadism, his scatology, and his necrophilia—proved to be in the service of other purposes. What did Fellini really want to say? All the evidence, in my view, points to the fact that Fellini wanted to re-present us to ourselves by helping us, compelling us to re-live critical phases in the experiences of Western men during the anguished hours of Rome's age-old history.

La Dolce Vita is the prelude to *The Satyricon.* Both are the working out of deeply committed experiments in Fellini's spiritual efforts to read our times. Knowing that Rome had been–and continues to be—one of the navels of the world, an irradiating nucleus of civilizational development, Fellini sought to depict a dilemma revealed by Rome's history. Fellini was sensitive to the fact that when Rome sought to be starkly pagan, it had a way of going berserk, out of its mind; when it sought to be altogether—

totally and totalistically—Christian, it became absurd. How does one get beyond this impasse? Fellini undertook an experiment: he tried to establish whether those who escaped being thrown off course by the distortions of the Christian sense of guilt, who hoped to be able to enjoy "pagan" innocence in their indulgences, are in fact able to manage to have joy without shame or whether the games they play destroy them.

I am now able to cite Fellini himself as a witness that my conjectures tally with the key facts. A recently published guide to Fellini's *Satyricon* permits us to read his own words. Interestingly, the setting of the interviews might almost be one from a Fellini film. A party is going on, starlets and international reporters are everywhere, and the renowned Moravia is one among them; he is the chief interviewer. Everyone explains Fellini to himself, but Fellini tells his own story clearly in his Preface. He explains he first read *The Satyricon* "many years ago at school," and that the reading remained a "vivid memory" and exerted "a constant and mysterious challenge." He continues:

> After the lapse of many years I reread the *Satyricon* recently . . .
> This time [there was] more than just a temptation to make a film out of it, there was a need, an enthusiastic certainty.
>   The encounter with that world and that society turned out to be a joyful affair, a stimulation of fantasy, an encounter rich in themes of remarkable relevance to modern society.[11]

Clearly, Fellini expects us to know that *La Dolce Vita* was for him a first step along this way. His remarks go forward to describe the "disconcerting analogies" between society today and Roman society "before the final arrival of Christianity."[12]

Fellini is quick to explain that his intentions went far beyond transcribing Petronius on film. His work was to be as much an experiment as a satire.

> . . . If the work of Petronius is the realistic, bloody and amusing description of the customs, characters and general feel of those times, the film we want to freely adapt from it could be a fresco in fantasy key, a powerful and evocative allegory—a satire of the world we live in today. Man never changes, and today we can recognise all the principal characters of the drama: Encolpius and Ascyltos, two hippy students, like any of those hanging around today in Piazza di Spagna, or in Paris, Amsterdam or London, moving on from adventure to adventure, even the most gruesome, without the least remorse, with all the natural innocence and splendid vitality of two young animals. Their revolt, though having

nothing in common with traditional revolts—neither the faith, nor the desperation, nor the drive to change or destroy—is nevertheless a revolt and is expressed in terms of utter ignorance of an estrangement from the society surrounding them. They live from day to day, taking problems as they come, their life interests alarmingly confined to the elementaries: they eat, make love, stick together, bed down anywhere. They make a living by the most haphazard expedients, often downright illegal ones. They are dropouts from every system, and recognize no obligations, duties or restrictions....

They are totally insensible to conventional ties like the family (usually built less on affection than on blackmail): they don't even practice the cult of friendship, which they consider a precarious and contradictory sentiment, and so are willing to betray or disown each other any time. They have no illusions precisely because they believe in nothing but, in a completely new and original way, their cynicism stays this side of a peaceful self-fulfillment, of a solid, healthy and unique good sense.[18]

That last remark offers Fellini's most compelling statement of the new credo. The new faith is expressed in the conviction that if previous structures of commitment, including commitment to one's dearest friends, are held in total abeyance, if there is a total rejection of any image of reciprocity, this may well be the very remedy which this dementing society apparently requires. Self-fulfillment then seems to be "solid, healthy and unique good sense."

Is this situation conceivable or possible? Has the new credo the makings of some new faith which will recover us from our alienation? The story fills out as we follow the details of the interview. On more than one occasion evidence develops that Moravia was not able to understand what Fellini was saying. Despite Moravia's vaunted moralism, he seems to enjoy the spectacle of ongoing decays. Fellini runs very much deeper. He reminds us here of Nietzsche! He explains:

When I think that at the time of Hadrian the cultivated, sensitive, cosmopolitan emperor who traveled constantly throughout the empire, in the Coliseums at Rome, one could witness the massacre of seventy-five pairs of gladiators in a single afternoon.... What escapes us in the mentality of the world in which you went to the box office or the theater and bought a ticket which entitled you to entertain yourself with the agony of a fellow human being killed by the sword or devoured by a wild beast. Death probably constituted the most entertaining part of these spectacles. People watched men die as today Spaniards watch bulls die: joking, laughing, having a drink.[14]

Moravia, ever the cultured critic, remarks, "Agony as a spectacle comes to an end in history with the coming of Christianity."

This seems to be as questionable an assertion as has been uttered in our century. Agony as a spectacle *does not come to an end in history with the coming of Christianity;* it takes myriad new forms. We, in our own time, are witnessing many of those forms. We, you and I, are able to look at our TV and see agonies far beyond the imagination of Roman proletarians and emperors alike, the agonies now occurring across the world which regularly appear on our TV screens—Vietnam, Biafra, East Pakistan, the agonies displayed in gladiatorial sport spectacles, football, and so on. Our films more than match the fantasies of de Sade.

It was the era of the late Middle Ages—in many ways a prototype of our times—which best understood that the games of life are the sources of the dances of death. The men of those days were fascinated by the image of the confrontation of the living and dead. Introducing a medieval dance of death, Florence Warren reminds us that the theme of the encounter of the three living and three dead occurs again and again. Actual dancing was frequently held at the times and places of death, and during the plague it was even encouraged as a means of raising people's spirits. There was a dance in which the dancers circled others who played dead. Death has an ironic and humorous tone, though there is the usual grim message underneath, for death takes liberties in addressing his subjects. He tells the abbot, for example, to dance "even though you're nothing light." The dance was jolly, and when it came time for each of the dancers to kiss their "dead" fellow goodbye, each would do an exaggerated parody of the act, which caused mirth. In the poem, "the grim confrontation of death with the living becomes a game of the living," Florence Warren explains.[15] (This last metaphor, introducing a moving variation of the image I had already selected for my own title, surprised me on running across it in Florence Warren's pages.)

Perhaps the most powerful explicit rendering of a medieval dance of death by a modern master will be found in Ingmar Bergman's *The Seventh Seal.* Indeed, the entire action of that great work occurs in an interlude or a reprieve between the sittings of a great game of chess, whose outcome the Knight-Crusader knows in advance: he will be checkmated by his opponent, Death. At the end, he learns that Death has "no secrets," "nothing to tell him." The central project under consideration among the people of the everyday world in interaction in the play is the planning of a re-presentation of the dance of death. Here again we have the links between the games of life and the dances of death.

As in the case of Fellini, we have Bergman's own word that the grim equations I have touched upon on these pages depict pangs and blights of modern existence. We dare not close our comparison of these two men, however, without remarking that a chasm seems to separate their images of world and future. Bergman sums up his own creed in the following stark lines:

> . . . In former days the artist remained unknown and his work was to the glory of God. He lived and died without being more or less important than other artisans; 'eternal values,' 'immortality' and 'masterpiece' were terms not applicable in his case. The ability to create was a gift. In such a world flourished invulnerable assurance and natural humility.
>
> Today the individual has become the highest form and the greatest bane of artistic creation. The smallest wound or pain of the ego is examined under a microscope as if it were of eternal importance. The artist considers his isolation, his subjectivity, his individualism almost holy. . . . The individualists stare into each other's eyes and yet deny the existence of each other. We walk in circles, so limited by our own anxieties that we can no longer distinguish between true and false, between the gangster's whim and the purest ideal.
>
> Thus if I am asked what I would like the general purpose of my films to be, I would reply that I want to be one of the artists in the cathedral on the great plain. I want to make a dragon's head, an angel, a devil—or perhaps a saint—out of stone. It does not matter which; it is the sense of satisfaction that counts. Regardless of whether I believe or not, whether I am a Christian or not, I would play my part in the collective building of the cathedral.[16]

I allow myself some summary theses on the *dramas* of life and death which constitute the fabrics of our several and joint histories. I do this by way of conclusion and reprise.

The present essay argues that societies do undergo changes in their images of their states of being; their senses of their past, present, and future; their experience of the balances of hoped-for fruitions and dreaded failures.[17] At times in the histories of societies, the tensions verge upon the unendurable. Deep confusion and perplexities begin to manifest themselves at every turn–in some as agony, in some as apathy, in some as effervescence, in some as immense urgency to engage in mindless acts of ecstasy, terror, fusion with others.

The most compelling instances or signs of the crisis state of civilization may be described as *anomie* and *vertigo*.[18] When this occurs, societies seem to be caught up in maelstrom. In the omnipresence of the grotesque,[19] all of the rules have been suspended and no longer appear to apply. A precedent seems to be absurd. Among the critical developments are new religious statements and truths allegedly derived from the sciences and the pseudosciences, that death has no power over man, that it is possible to eliminate it by the expansion of consciousness or by some particular device of a new science or an old science, whether it be reincarnation or cryonic suspension.[20] Whenever societies are close to the state of vertigo, we discover the increase of frenzied efforts to fight off the sense of impending doom. Vast numbers of people are propelled into violent motions, whether in dance, marathon,[21] nomadism, or in brutal sports of an agonistic character.

The most interesting of all of the responses of individuals and groups to the sense of impending doom is the increase in pressure to create games and dances which distract one's mind from brooding over one's fate. I have called these games "the games of life," and when they are looked at very carefully, it is observed that these games of life, whose purpose one would suppose would be to stave off the dances of death are after their own fashion, dances of death; for, in the playing of the games of life, we actually lose our lives or cast them away in one or another fashion.

The connections between the games of life and the dances of death were very well understood by men of another time, especially the men of the Middle Ages. It is, therefore, no wonder whatever that they gave so much stress to the idea of the dances of death. Indeed, these were always projected as the games of life which were being played by hectic and frenzied dancers.[22]

The stuff which we produce as "plays" in our theaters is the dramas of our lives and deaths. Who does not relive these histories will not be able to reappropriate these re-presentations. We are the authors, the audience, the actors, and the acts. The stories we are telling and are being told are about ourselves.[23]

De nobis fabulae narrantur.

NOTES

---

1. T. S. Eliot, "The Hollow Men," in, *The Collected Poems: 1909–1962.* (New York: Harcourt, Brace, Jovanovich, 1962, 1st pub. 1925). Reprinted by permission of Harcourt Brace Jovanovich.

Clues to the wider perspectives adopted in this essay will be found in the writings of Durkheim, Jane Harrison, Johan Huizinga, and others who place strong stress on the structures of experience in the shaping of men's expressions. See esp., Emile Durkheim, *The*

Elementary Forms of the Religious Life, tr. by J. W. Swain (London: Allen & Unwin, 1915, 1st pub. 1912). Jane Harrison, *Themis* (Cambridge: Cambridge University Press, 1912), reprinted in, *Epilogomena to the Study of Greek Religion and Themis: A Study of the Social Origins of Greek Religion* (New Hyde Park, NY: University Books, 1962). J. Huizinga, *The Waning of the Middle Ages* (New York: Longmans, Green, 1924). Also see some earlier essays: Benjamin Nelson, "Genet's *The Balcony* and Parisian Existentialism," *Tulane Drama Review* 7 (1963):60–79. "Actors, Directors, Roles, Cues, Meanings, Identities: Further Thoughts on 'Anomie'," *Psychoanalytic Review* 51 (1964):135–160. "Preface," in G. Rosen, *Madness in Society: Chapters in the Historical Sociology of Mental Illness* (Chicago: University of Chicago Press, 1969). "The Omnipresence of the Grotesque," *Psychoanalytic Review* 57 (1972):505–518.

2. The evanescence of civilizations has rarely been rendered as poignantly as in Paul Valery's "Crisis of the Mind," in Paul Valery, *History and Politics*, tr. by D. Folliot and J. Matthews (New York: Pantheon, 1962, 1st publ. 1919). A striking contrast to Valery's view of civilization will be found in Robert Nisbet, *Social Change and History* (New York: Oxford University Press, 1969), p. 3, but cf. Benjamin Nelson, "Metaphor in Sociology," review of Nisbet's *Social Change and History*, in *Science Magazine* 166 (Dec. 19, 1969):1498–1500.

3. S. Dill, *Roman Society: The Last Century of the Western Empire* (New York: Meridian, 1957, 1st publ. 1898).

4. Dill, Book V, c. 1, *passim*, esp. pp. 415, 428–429. On the Christian side, see the earlier exceptional work: Salvianus of Marseilles, *On the Government of God*, tr. from the Latin by E. M. Sanford (New York: Columbia University Press, 1930, 1st publ. 439–450 A.D.). Also see Dill, pp. 137–141.

5. Huizinga, *The Waning of the Middle Ages*.

6. Somerset Maugham, *Of Human Bondage* (New York: Modern Library, 1930), pp. 263–64. Reprinted by permission of Random House from Vintage edition, 1956.

7. Arthur Rimbaud, *A Season in Hell*, tr. by L. Varese (Norforlk: Laughlin, 1961, 1st pub. 1873).

8. This scheme is given insistent stress in the script written for—and acted by—Beckett's friend, Jack McGowran.

9. Cyrus Day, "The Iceman and the Bridegroom: Some Observations on the Death of O'Neill's Salesman," in, J. H. Raleigh, ed., *Twentieth-Century Interpretations of The Iceman Cometh* (Englewood Cliffs, N.J.: Prentice-Hall, 1968), p. 83.

10. Karl Schiftgriesser concludes an interview with O'Neill saying, "But as it (the play) proceeds, the 'Iceman' who started as a ribald joke, takes on a different, deeper and even terrifying meaning and before the end becomes Death itself," in Raleigh, ed., p. 28.

11. F. Fellini, *Satyricon*, ed. by Dario Zanelli, tr. by E. Walter and J. Matthews (New York: Ballantine, 1970), p. 43. Reprinted by permission of Ballantine Books.

12. Fellini, *Satyricon*, p. 43. As this essay goes to press, word comes from Italy that Fellini has now completed a new film entitled *Roma: The Decline of the Roman Empire, 1931–1972*.

13. Fellini, *Satyricon*, p. 44.

14. Fellini, *Satyricon*, p. 26.

15. Florence Warren, ed., *The Dance of Death*. Collected from mss. by F. Warren. Intro. and notes by Beatrice White, tr. by William Lydgate (Early English Text Society, Original Series, no. 181).

16. I. Bergman, *The Seventh Seal: A Film* (New York: Simon & Schuster, 1960). Reprinted by permission of Simon & Schuster.

17. Benjamin Nelson, "*Eros, Logos, Nomos, Polis*: Their Changing Balances in the Vicissitudes of Communities and Civilizations," in Alan Eister, ed., *Changing Perspectives in the Scientific Study of Religion* (New York: Wiley-Interscience, 1974), pp. 85–111.

18. Durkheim, *The Elementary Forms.* R. K. Merton, "Social Structure and Anomie," in R. K. Merton, *Social Theory & Social Structure* (New York: Free Press, 1968), pp. 131–161. Nelson, "Actors, Directors, Roles, Cues, Meanings."

19. Nelson, "The Omnipresence of the Grotesque."

20. Evidence indicates that the key source of this movement is the 1964 book by Robert Ettinger, *The Prospect of Immortality* (Garden City: Doubleday, 1964). An exceptionally interesting recent case is described in Bill Barry, "Playing It Cold," *Newsday* (Long Island, New York, Nov. 12, 1971), pp. 7W–15W.

21. Robert Coates offers the following "Afterword" to Horace McCoy's novel, *They Shoot Horses, Don't They?* (New York: Avon, 1966):

> The dance marathon was truly a *danse macabre*, and the violent contrasts inherent in the scene: the band (always, as the author notes, playing, overly loud), the gaudy festoons and ribbons of bunting strung all over the hall, the bars and hot dog counters along the walls, the intermittently booming loud speakers, all centering on the weaving array of close-to-collapsing contestants, almost literally walking in their sleep—these contrasts only served to heighten the resemblance to a kind of Surrealist, latter-day Inferno. (All this too was punctuated—and this the author brings out skillfully indeed—by the fiendish jocularity of the promoter, who was always at his most expansive when he was ordering an extra sprint to thin out some of the contestants.)

See Jonathan Eisen's review of R. Neville's study of the "international underground" of "play power", in Jonathan Eisen, "Selling the Underground," *Book World* (Jan. 10, 1971).

22. E. Louis Backman, *Religious Dances in the Christian Church and Popular Medicine*, tr. by E. Classen (London: Allen & Unwin, 1952).

23. Benjamin Nelson, "Genet's *The Balcony* and Parisian Existentialism." "Actors, Directors, Roles, Cues, Meanings." "The Omnipresence of the Grotesque." "Myths, Mysteries and Milieux," presented to the Annual Congress of Fellows, *Society for the Arts, Religion and Contemporary Culture*, New York, Feb. 26, 1972. Michel Foucault, *Madness in Civilization: A History of Insanity in the Age of Reason* (New York: Pantheon, 1965).